ANSWERS—WHO KNOWS ONE

I know one—God is One.
I know two—Two are the Tables of the Covenant.
I know three—Three Patriarchs: Abraham, Isaac, Jacob.
I know four—Four Matriarchs: Sarah, Rebecca, Rachel, Leah.
I know five—Five Books of Moses: Genesis, Exodus, Leviticus, Numbers, Deuteronomy.
I know six—Six are the sections of the Mishnah.
I know seven—Seven days of the week.
I know eight—Eight are the days to circumcision.
I know nine—Nine are the months to childbirth.
I know ten—Ten are the Ten Commandments:

1. I am Adonai thy God.
2. You shall have no other gods before Me.
3. You shalt not take the name of Adonai your God in vain.
4. Remember the Sabbath Day.
5. Honor your father and your mother.
6. You shall not murder.
7. You shall not commit adultery.
8. You shall not steal.
9. You shall not bear false witness.
10. You shall not covet.

I know eleven—Eleven are the stars in Josph's dream. The stars were symbolic of the brothers who would one day bow down to him.
I know twelve—Twelve tribes in Israel:

Reuben	Issachar	Dan
Shimon	Zebulun	Naftali
Levi	Benjamin	Gad
Yehudah		Asher
Joseph (Ephraim and Manasseh)		

I know thirteen—Thirteen are the attributes of God listed in Exodus 34:6-7.

MOSES AND THE LAMB

Moses fled from Egypt to the country of Midian. Here he became a shepherd for a priest called Jethro.

One day, as Moses was caring for the sheep, a little lamb wandered away from the flock. Our wise men tell us that Moses went in search of it and found it far away. Tenderly, Moses lifted the lamb to his shoulder and carried it back to the flock.

God saw how Moses loved and cared for even the smallest of Jethro's lambs. God said: "Here, indeed, is a good shepherd for My people."

THE SABBATH IN EGYPT

The Egyptian Pharaoh was afraid the Hebrews would increase and grow strong and rule over the land. So he made them work seven days a week as slaves.

Our wise men tell us that Moses was filled with sorrow when he saw his people working so hard. He went to the Pharaoh and said: "Let your slaves rest every seventh day. Then they will work even harder the other six days."

The Pharaoh listened to this advice. Thus, even when they were slaves in Egypt, the Hebrews celebrated the Sabbath.

THE RED SEA

When the Children of Israel reached the Red Sea, God said to Moses: "Lift your rod above the sea. I will send a great wind to part the waters and make a dry path for My people."

Moses could have led the Israelites around the Red Sea. Then why did God command him to lead them across it?

Our wise men tell us that God wanted to punish the Egyptians and prove to them that the Lord's power was greater than any power on earth

And so the Israelites crossed the Red Sea safely, while the wicked Egyptian soldiers following them were drowned.

THE DAY THE ANGELS STOPPED SINGING

Our wise men tell us that every day the angels of heaven sing praises to God. But on one day, they were silent. God had commanded them not to sing.

This was the day Moses led the Children of Israel across the Red Sea. Behind them came the cruel Egyptian soldiers. When the Hebrews reached the other side, God made the waters close over the heads of the soldiers.

"Even though the Egyptians are wicked," God told the angels, "they are still My creatures. I cannot listen to your singing when My own creatures are drowning in the sea." Great is God's love for all living things.

THE PHARAOH'S PALACE

Our wise men tell us that the Pharaoh of Egypt lived in a mighty palace, guarded by wild and ferocious beasts. When people tried to enter the palace gates, these beasts leaped at them and drove them away in terror.

One day, two men came to the palace gates. One was Aaron, brother of Moses, and the other was Moses himself. They came to ask the Pharaoh to free the Hebrews from slavery.

Moses and Aaron walked bravely up to the gates where the fierce beasts roared. Lo and behold! The animals became as tame as kittens. They licked Aaron's and Moses' hands, and the two Hebrew leaders walked through the gates unharmed.

THE TAMBOURINES

When Moses led the Hebrews out of Egypt, the people left in such a hurry that they did not even have time to bake their bread. They quickly gathered up the unleavened dough and fled.

Our wise men tell us that in spite of their great hurry, there was one thing they remembered to take. Every Hebrew woman brought along her tambourine.

So great was their faith that God would save them that they wanted to have their tambourines with them to celebrate their freedom with joyful singing and music.

MOSES THE STUTTERER

Moses was a beautiful child. The princess loved baby Moses very much. She would spend her days playing with the baby.

The Pharaoh was also very fond of baby Moses. He would hold the baby on his lap and allow Moses to take the shiny golden crown from his head and play with it.

The Egyptian priests warned Pharaoh that this was a sign that someday Moses would take the Kingdom of Egypt away from him. The priests were so sure that they even suggested killing the baby. Pharaoh and his daughter refused to listen to their advice.

Finally, Pharaoh agreed to test the child. The priests placed a plate with a golden bar and a hot coal in front of baby Moses. If he picked up the gold, it would mean that he understood exactly what he was doing, and then he would be killed.

If the baby chose the hot coal, that would mean that he did not know what he was doing, and then he would remain alive.

The plate was placed before Moses. He reached for the shiny gold bar, but an angel moved his hand to the hot coal.

Moses picked up the burning coal and placed it on his lips. His tongue was burned and he became a stutterer. Moses' life was saved, and later on he freed his people from Egyptian slavery.

FROM THE MIDRASH

BIRTH OF MOSES

"A son will be born to my mother and father who will deliver Israel from Egypt." Our wise men tell us that this was the prophecy made by Miriam, sister of Moses.

When Moses was born, his tiny face shone with a bright, heavenly light. Then his parents knew that what Miriam had prophesied would come to pass.

The prophecy was fulfilled when, many years later, Moses led the Children of Israel out of Egypt to the Promised Land.

THE EGYPTIAN PRINCESS

The daughter of the Pharaoh went to bathe in the river Nile with her servants. There, hidden in the bushes, they found the baby Moses in a basket.

The princess took the baby to the palace and raised him as her own son.

Why did the Princess and her maidens go bathing on that particular day? Our wise men tell us it was because God made that day as scorching hot as a furnace. The Lord wanted Moses to be found so that he could grow up to be a great leader for his people.

דְּזַבִּן אַבָּא בִּתְרֵי זוּזֵי.	My father bought for two zuzim.
חַד גַּדְיָא. חַד גַּדְיָא.	*One little goat, had gadya.*
וַאֲתָא תוֹרָא.	Then came an ox
וְשָׁתָה לְמַיָּא. דְּכָבָה לְנוּרָא.	And drank the water that put out the fire
דְּשָׂרַף לְחוּטְרָא. דְּהִכָּה לְכַלְבָּא.	That burned the stick that beat the dog
דְּנָשַׁךְ לְשׁוּנְרָא. דְּאָכְלָה לְגַדְיָא.	That bit the cat that ate the goat
דְּזַבִּן אַבָּא בִּתְרֵי זוּזֵי.	My father bought for two zuzim.
חַד גַּדְיָא. חַד גַּדְיָא.	*One little goat, had gadya.*
וַאֲתָא הַשּׁוֹחֵט. וְשָׁחַט לְתוֹרָא.	Then came a *shohet* and slaughtered the ox,
דְּשָׁתָה לְמַיָּא. דְּכָבָה לְנוּרָא.	That drank the water that put out the fire
דְּשָׂרַף לְחוּטְרָא. דְּהִכָּה לְכַלְבָּא.	That burned the stick that beat the dog
דְּנָשַׁךְ לְשׁוּנְרָא. דְּאָכְלָה לְגַדְיָא.	That bit the cat that ate the goat
דְּזַבִּן אַבָּא בִּתְרֵי זוּזֵי.	My father bought for two zuzim.
חַד גַּדְיָא. חַד גַּדְיָא.	*One little goat, had gadya*
וַאֲתָא מַלְאַךְ הַמָּוֶת.	Then came the Angel of Death
וְשָׁחַט לְשׁוֹחֵט דְּשָׁחַט לְתוֹרָא.	And killed the *shohet* that slaughtered the ox
דְּשָׁתָה לְמַיָּא. דְּכָבָה לְנוּרָא.	That drank the water that put out the fire
דְּשָׂרַף לְחוּטְרָא. דְּהִכָּה לְכַלְבָּא.	That burned the stick that beat the dog
דְּנָשַׁךְ לְשׁוּנְרָא. דְּאָכְלָה לְגַדְיָא.	That bit the cat that ate the goat
דְּזַבִּן אַבָּא בִּתְרֵי זוּזֵי.	My father bought for two zuzim
חַד גַּדְיָא. חַד גַּדְיָא.	*One little goat, had gadya.*
וַאֲתָא הַקָּדוֹשׁ בָּרוּךְ הוּא.	Then came the Holy One
וְשָׁחַט לְמַלְאַךְ הַמָּוֶת.	And slew the angel of death
דְּשָׁחַט לְשׁוֹחֵט. דְּשָׁחַט לְתוֹרָא.	Who killed the *shohet* who slaughtered the ox
דְּשָׁתָה לְמַיָּא. דְּכָבָה לְנוּרָא,	That drank the water that put out the fire
דְּשָׂרַף לְחוּטְרָא. דְּהִכָּה לְכַלְבָּא.	That burned the stick that beat the dog
דְּנָשַׁךְ לְשׁוּנְרָא. דְּאָכְלָה לְגַדְיָא.	That bit the cat that ate the goat
דְּזַבִּן אַבָּא בִּתְרֵי זוּזֵי.	My father bought for two zuzim.
חַד גַּדְיָא. חַד גַּדְיָא:	*One little goat, had gadya.*

HAD GADYA - AN ONLY GOAT

This rhythmic folk song describes the unhappy adventure of a little goat, **had gadya,** purchased for two **zuzim** (coins) by a kind father for his child.

In this parable we read the story of the Jewish people. Each and every time a new power rises by force of arms. The song ends with an expression of hope: Then came the Almighty bringing peace to the world.

One little goat, one little goat,
חַד גַּדְיָא. חַד גַּדְיָא.

דְּזַבַּן אַבָּא בִּתְרֵי זוּזֵי. — My father bought for two zuzim.
חַד גַּדְיָא. חַד גַּדְיָא. — *One little goat, had gadya.*

וְאָתָא שׁוּנְרָא. וְאָכְלָה לְגַדְיָא. — Then came a cat and ate the goat
דְּזַבַּן אַבָּא בִּתְרֵי זוּזֵי. — My father bought for two zuzim.
חַד גַּדְיָא. חַד גַּדְיָא. — *One little goat, had gadya.*

וְאָתָא כַלְבָּא. וְנָשַׁךְ לְשׁוּנְרָא. — Then came a dog and bit the cat
דְּאָכְלָה לְגַדְיָא. — That ate the goat
דְּזַבַּן אַבָּא בִּתְרֵי זוּזֵי. — My father bought for two zuzim.
חַד גַּדְיָא. חַד גַּדְיָא. — *One little goat, had gadya.*

וְאָתָא חוּטְרָא. וְהִכָּה לְכַלְבָּא. — Then came a stick and beat the dog
דְּנָשַׁךְ לְשׁוּנְרָא. דְּאָכְלָה לְגַדְיָא. — That bit the cat that ate the goat
דְּזַבַּן אַבָּא בִּתְרֵי זוּזֵי. — My father bought for two zuzim.
חַד גַּדְיָא. חַד גַּדְיָא. — *One little goat, had gadya.*

וְאָתָא נוּרָא. — Then came a fire
וְשָׂרַף לְחוּטְרָא. דְּהִכָּה לְכַלְבָּא. — And burned the stick that beat the dog
דְּנָשַׁךְ לְשׁוּנְרָא. דְּאָכְלָה לְגַדְיָא. — That bit the cat that ate the goat
דְּזַבַּן אַבָּא בִּתְרֵי זוּזֵי. — My father bought for two zuzim.
חַד גַּדְיָא. חַד גַּדְיָא. — *One little goat, had gadya.*

וְאָתָא מַיָּא. וְכָבָה לְנוּרָא. — Then came the water and put out the fire
דְּשָׂרַף לְחוּטְרָא. דְּהִכָּה לְכַלְבָּא. — That burned the stick that beat the dog
דְּנָשַׁךְ לְשׁוּנְרָא. דְּאָכְלָה לְגַדְיָא. — That bit the cat that ate the goat

Who knows eleven?

I know eleven—Eleven are the stars of Joseph's dream.
Ten are the commandments at Sinai.
Nine are the months to childbirth.
Eight are the days to circumcision.
Seven are the days of the week.
Six are the sections of the Mishnah.
Five are the books of the Torah.
Four are the matriarchs.
Three are the patriarchs.
Two are the tablets of the covenant.
One is our God in heaven and on earth.

אַחַד עָשָׂר מִי יוֹדֵעַ?

אַחַד עָשָׂר אֲנִי יוֹדֵעַ. אַחַד עָשָׂר כּוֹכְבַיָּא. עֲשָׂרָה דִבְּרַיָּא. תִּשְׁעָה יַרְחֵי לֵדָה. שְׁמוֹנָה יְמֵי מִילָה. שִׁבְעָה יְמֵי שַׁבַּתָּא. שִׁשָּׁה סִדְרֵי מִשְׁנָה. חֲמִשָּׁה חוּמְשֵׁי תוֹרָה. אַרְבַּע אִמָּהוֹת. שְׁלֹשָׁה אָבוֹת. שְׁנֵי לֻחוֹת הַבְּרִית. אֶחָד אֱלֹהֵינוּ שֶׁבַּשָּׁמַיִם וּבָאָרֶץ.

Who knows twelve?

I know twelve—Twelve are the tribes of Israel.
Eleven are the stars of Joseph's dream.
Ten are the commandments at Sinai.
Nine are the months to childbirth.
Eight are the days to circumcision.
Seven are the days of the week.
Six are the sections of the Mishnah.
Five are the books of the Torah.
Four are the matriarchs.
Three are the patriarchs.
Two are the tablets of the covenant.
One is our God in heaven and on earth.

שְׁנֵים עָשָׂר מִי יוֹדֵעַ?

שְׁנֵים עָשָׂר אֲנִי יוֹדֵעַ. שְׁנֵים עָשָׂר שִׁבְטַיָּא. אַחַד עָשָׂר כּוֹכְבַיָּא. עֲשָׂרָה דִבְּרַיָּא. תִּשְׁעָה יַרְחֵי לֵדָה. שְׁמוֹנָה יְמֵי מִילָה. שִׁבְעָה יְמֵי שַׁבַּתָּא. שִׁשָּׁה סִדְרֵי מִשְׁנָה. חֲמִשָּׁה חוּמְשֵׁי תוֹרָה. אַרְבַּע אִמָּהוֹת. שְׁלֹשָׁה אָבוֹת. שְׁנֵי לֻחוֹת הַבְּרִית. אֶחָד אֱלֹהֵינוּ שֶׁבַּשָּׁמַיִם וּבָאָרֶץ.

Who knows thirteen?

I know thirteen—Thirteen are the qualities of God.
Twelve are the tribes of Israel.
Eleven are the stars of Joseph's dream.
Ten are the commandments at Sinai.
Nine are the months to childbirth.
Eight are the days to circumcision.
Seven are the days of the week.
Six are the sections of the Mishnah.
Five are the books of the Torah.
Four are the matriarchs.
Three are the patriarchs.
Two are the tablets of the covenant.
One is our God in heaven and on earth.

שְׁלֹשָׁה עָשָׂר מִי יוֹדֵעַ?

שְׁלֹשָׁה עָשָׂר אֲנִי יוֹדֵעַ. שְׁלֹשָׁה עָשָׂר מִדַּיָּא. שְׁנֵים עָשָׂר שִׁבְטַיָּא. אַחַד עָשָׂר כּוֹכְבַיָּא. עֲשָׂרָה דִבְּרַיָּא. תִּשְׁעָה יַרְחֵי לֵדָה. שְׁמוֹנָה יְמֵי מִילָה. שִׁבְעָה יְמֵי שַׁבַּתָּא. שִׁשָּׁה סִדְרֵי מִשְׁנָה. חֲמִשָּׁה חוּמְשֵׁי תוֹרָה. אַרְבַּע אִמָּהוֹת. שְׁלֹשָׁה אָבוֹת. שְׁנֵי לֻחוֹת הַבְּרִית. אֶחָד אֱלֹהֵינוּ שֶׁבַּשָּׁמַיִם וּבָאָרֶץ.

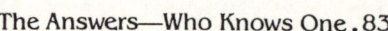

The Answers—Who Knows One, 83

Who knows seven? שִׁבְעָה מִי יוֹדֵעַ?

שִׁבְעָה אֲנִי יוֹדֵעַ. שִׁבְעָה יְמֵי שַׁבַּתָּא. שִׁשָּׁה סִדְרֵי מִשְׁנָה. חֲמִשָּׁה חוּמְשֵׁי תוֹרָה. אַרְבַּע אִמָּהוֹת. שְׁלֹשָׁה אָבוֹת. שְׁנֵי לֻחוֹת הַבְּרִית. אֶחָד אֱלֹהֵינוּ שֶׁבַּשָּׁמַיִם וּבָאָרֶץ.

I know seven—Seven are the days of the week.
    Six are the sections of the Mishnah
    Five are the books of the Torah.
    Four are the matriarchs.
    Three are the patriarchs.
    Two are the tablets of the covenant.
    One is our God in heaven and on earth.

Who knows eight? שְׁמוֹנָה מִי יוֹדֵעַ?

שְׁמוֹנָה אֲנִי יוֹדֵעַ. שְׁמוֹנָה יְמֵי מִילָה. שִׁבְעָה יְמֵי שַׁבַּתָּא. שִׁשָּׁה סִדְרֵי מִשְׁנָה. חֲמִשָּׁה חוּמְשֵׁי תוֹרָה. אַרְבַּע אִמָּהוֹת. שְׁלֹשָׁה אָבוֹת. שְׁנֵי לֻחוֹת הַבְּרִית. אֶחָד אֱלֹהֵינוּ שֶׁבַּשָּׁמַיִם וּבָאָרֶץ.

I know eight—Eight are the days to circumcision.
    Seven are the days of the week.
    Six are the sections of the Mishnah.
    Five are the books of the Torah.
    Four are the matriarchs.
    Three are the patriarchs.
    Two are the tablets of the covenant.
    One is our God in heaven and on earth.

Who knows nine תִּשְׁעָה מִי יוֹדֵעַ?

תִּשְׁעָה אֲנִי יוֹדֵעַ. תִּשְׁעָה יַרְחֵי לֵדָה. שְׁמוֹנָה יְמֵי מִילָה. שִׁבְעָה יְמֵי שַׁבַּתָּא. שִׁשָּׁה סִדְרֵי מִשְׁנָה. חֲמִשָּׁה חוּמְשֵׁי תוֹרָה. אַרְבַּע אִמָּהוֹת. שְׁלֹשָׁה אָבוֹת. שְׁנֵי לֻחוֹת הַבְּרִית. אֶחָד אֱלֹהֵינוּ שֶׁבַּשָּׁמַיִם וּבָאָרֶץ.

I know nine—Nine are the months to childbirth.
    Eight are the days to circumcision.
    Seven are the days of the week.
    Six are the sections of the Mishnah.
    Five are the books of the Torah.
    Four are the matriarchs.
    Three are the patriarchs.
    Two are the tablets of the covenant.
    One is our God in heaven and on earth.

Who knows ten? עֲשָׂרָה מִי יוֹדֵעַ?

עֲשָׂרָה אֲנִי יוֹדֵעַ. עֲשָׂרָה דִבְּרַיָּא. תִּשְׁעָה יַרְחֵי לֵדָה. שְׁמוֹנָה יְמֵי מִילָה. שִׁבְעָה יְמֵי שַׁבַּתָּא. שִׁשָּׁה סִדְרֵי מִשְׁנָה. חֲמִשָּׁה חוּמְשֵׁי תוֹרָה. אַרְבַּע אִמָּהוֹת. שְׁלֹשָׁה אָבוֹת. שְׁנֵי לֻחוֹת הַבְּרִית. אֶחָד אֱלֹהֵינוּ שֶׁבַּשָּׁמַיִם וּבָאָרֶץ.

I know ten—Ten are the commandments at Sinai.
    Nine are the months to childbirth.
    Eight are the days to circumcision.
    Seven are the days of the week.
    Six are the sections of the Mishnah.
    Five are the books of the Torah.
    Four are the matriarchs.
    Three are the patriarchs.
    Two are the tablets of the covenant.
    One is our God in heaven and on earth.

EHAD ME YODEAH
WHO KNOWS ONE?

"Who Knows One" is a riddle song, as well as a short course in Jewish history and customs. Who knows one, who knows two, who knows three. Do you know the answer? If you don't, see page 83.

אֶחָד מִי יוֹדֵעַ?
אֶחָד אֲנִי יוֹדֵעַ.
אֶחָד אֱלֹהֵינוּ שֶׁבַּשָּׁמַיִם וּבָאָרֶץ.

Who knows one?
I know one—One is our God in heaven and on earth.
Ehad eloheinu sheh-ba-shamayim u-va-aretz.

שְׁנַיִם מִי יוֹדֵעַ?
שְׁנַיִם אֲנִי יוֹדֵעַ. שְׁנֵי לֻחוֹת הַבְּרִית.
אֶחָד אֱלֹהֵינוּ שֶׁבַּשָּׁמַיִם וּבָאָרֶץ.

Who knows two?
I know two—Two are the tablets of the covenant.
One is our God in heaven and on earth.

שְׁלֹשָׁה מִי יוֹדֵעַ?
שְׁלֹשָׁה אֲנִי יוֹדֵעַ. שְׁלֹשָׁה אָבוֹת.
שְׁנֵי לֻחוֹת הַבְּרִית.
אֶחָד אֱלֹהֵינוּ שֶׁבַּשָּׁמַיִם וּבָאָרֶץ.

Who knows three?
I know three—Three are the patriarchs.
Two are the tablets of the covenant.
One is our God in heaven and on earth.

אַרְבַּע מִי יוֹדֵעַ?
אַרְבַּע אֲנִי יוֹדֵעַ. אַרְבַּע אִמָּהוֹת.
שְׁלֹשָׁה אָבוֹת. שְׁנֵי לֻחוֹת הַבְּרִית.
אֶחָד אֱלֹהֵינוּ שֶׁבַּשָּׁמַיִם וּבָאָרֶץ.

Who knows four?
I know four—Four are the matriarchs.
Three are the patriarchs.
Two are the tablets of the covenant.
One is our God in heaven and on earth.

חֲמִשָּׁה מִי יוֹדֵעַ?
חֲמִשָּׁה אֲנִי יוֹדֵעַ. חֲמִשָּׁה חוּמְשֵׁי תוֹרָה
אַרְבַּע אִמָּהוֹת. שְׁלֹשָׁה אָבוֹת.
שְׁנֵי לֻחוֹת הַבְּרִית.
אֶחָד אֱלֹהֵינוּ שֶׁבַּשָּׁמַיִם וּבָאָרֶץ.

Who knows five?
I know five—Five are the books of the Torah.
Four are the matriarchs.
Three are the patriarchs.
Two are the tablets of the covenant.
One is our God in heaven and on earth.

שִׁשָּׁה מִי יוֹדֵעַ?
שִׁשָּׁה אֲנִי יוֹדֵעַ. שִׁשָּׁה סִדְרֵי מִשְׁנָה.
חֲמִשָּׁה חוּמְשֵׁי תוֹרָה.
אַרְבַּע אִמָּהוֹת. שְׁלֹשָׁה אָבוֹת.
שְׁנֵי לֻחוֹת הַבְּרִית.
אֶחָד אֱלֹהֵינוּ שֶׁבַּשָּׁמַיִם וּבָאָרֶץ.

Who knows six?
I know six—Six are the sections of the Mishnah.
Five are the books of the Torah.
Four are the matriarchs.
Three are the patriarchs.
Two are the tablets of the covenant.
One is our God in heaven and on earth.

PASSOVER SONGS

During the Seder we sing lots of songs. Some are songs of thanks to God for saving our people in Egypt. Some are fun songs. Everyone at the Seder sings and everyone has a good time.

The Jewish people all over the world are like one large family. We have the same mitzvot. We celebrate the same holidays. Jews in Africa, Asia, Israel, or Europe all celebrate the same holiday of Passover. All of us read the same prayers and sing the same Passover songs. Why do we sing so much at the Seder? Because slaves are always working and are not allowed to rest or sing. We are free, so we sing with joy.

God is mighty.

אַדִיר הוּא.

יִבְנֶה בֵיתוֹ בְּקָרוֹב.
בִּמְהֵרָה בִּמְהֵרָה, בְּיָמֵינוּ בְּקָרוֹב.
אֵל בְּנֵה. אֵל בְּנֵה.
בְּנֵה בֵיתְךָ בְּקָרוֹב:

בָּחוּר הוּא. גָּדוֹל הוּא.
דָּגוּל הוּא. יִבְנֶה בֵיתוֹ בְּקָרוֹב.
בִּמְהֵרָה בִּמְהֵרָה, בְּיָמֵינוּ בְּקָרוֹב.
אֵל בְּנֵה. אֵל בְּנֵה. בְּנֵה בֵיתְךָ בְּקָרוֹב:

הָדוּר הוּא. וָתִיק הוּא.
זַכַּאי הוּא. חָסִיד הוּא.
יִבְנֶה בֵיתוֹ בְּקָרוֹב.
בִּמְהֵרָה בִּמְהֵרָה, בְּיָמֵינוּ בְּקָרוֹב.
אֵל בְּנֵה. אֵל בְּנֵה.
בְּנֵה בֵיתְךָ בְּקָרוֹב:

טָהוֹר הוּא. יָחִיד הוּא.
כַּבִּיר הוּא. לָמוּד הוּא.

מֶלֶךְ הוּא. נוֹרָא הוּא.
סַגִּיב הוּא. עִזּוּז הוּא.
פּוֹדֶה הוּא. צַדִּיק הוּא.
יִבְנֶה בֵיתוֹ בְּקָרוֹב.
בִּמְהֵרָה בִּמְהֵרָה, בְּיָמֵינוּ בְּקָרוֹב.
אֵל בְּנֵה. אֵל בְּנֵה.
בְּנֵה בֵיתְךָ בְּקָרוֹב.

קָדוֹשׁ הוּא. רַחוּם הוּא.
שַׁדַּי הוּא. תַּקִּיף הוּא.
יִבְנֶה בֵיתוֹ בְּקָרוֹב.
בִּמְהֵרָה בִּמְהֵרָה, בְּיָמֵינוּ בְּקָרוֹב.
אֵל בְּנֵה. אֵל בְּנֵה.
בְּנֵה בֵיתְךָ בְּקָרוֹב.

The poem Adir Hu is an acrostic. Beginning with the letter Alef א in אַדִיר Adir, the adjectives are in alphabetical order. See if you can find the alphabet.

NEXT YEAR IN JERUSALEM

We end the Seder with the Hebrew words L'Shanah HaBaah Berushalayim.

Next year in Jerusalem.

Our people began in the land of Israel thousands of years ago. Our people loved the land of Israel. They used to say that Israel was the center of the world. And right in the middle of Israel was Jerusalem and the Holy Temple.

But almost two thousand years ago, most of the Jews were driven out of Israel.

Then, in 1948, after much fighting, the State of Israel was set up once again. Once again Israel is free. Once again the holy city of Jerusalem is the capital of Israel.

לְשָׁנָה הַבָּאָה בִּירוּשָׁלָיִם:

Next year in Jerusalem.

THE FOURTH CUP OF WINE

We now recite the blessing and drink the fourth and last cup of wine. This cup of wine recalls God's fourth promise, "I choose you to be My people."

Recite the blessing and drink the fourth cup of wine.

בָּרוּךְ אַתָּה יְיָ, **Blessed is Adonai,**
אֱלֹהֵינוּ מֶלֶךְ הָעוֹלָם, our God, ruler of the world,
בּוֹרֵא פְּרִי הַגָּפֶן. who created the fruit of the vine.

נִרְצָה
NIRTZAH

The End of the Service

This is the fourteenth and last ceremony of the Passover Seder.

חֲסַל סִדּוּר פֶּסַח **The Passover Seder**
כְּהִלְכָתוֹ. **is ended.**
בְּכָל מִשְׁפָּטוֹ וְחֻקָּתוֹ. According to Jewish custom and law.
כַּאֲשֶׁר זָכִינוּ, לְסַדֵּר אוֹתוֹ, We celebrated it now,
כֵּן נִזְכֶּה לַעֲשׂוֹתוֹ. may we celebrate it
for many years to come.

כִּי לוֹ נָאֶה. To God praise is fitting.
כִּי לוֹ יָאֶה. To God praise is due.

אַדִּיר בִּמְלוּכָה.	מוֹשֵׁל בִּמְלוּכָה.
בָּחוּר כַּהֲלָכָה.	נוֹרָא כַּהֲלָכָה.
גְּדוּדָיו יֹאמְרוּ לוֹ.	סְבִיבָיו יֹאמְרוּ לוֹ.
לְךָ וּלְךָ. לְךָ כִּי לְךָ.	לְךָ וּלְךָ. לְךָ כִּי לְךָ.
לְךָ אַף לְךָ. לְךָ יְיָ הַמַּמְלָכָה.	לְךָ אַף לְךָ. לְךָ יְיָ הַמַּמְלָכָה.
כִּי לוֹ נָאֶה. כִּי לוֹ יָאֶה.	כִּי לוֹ נָאֶה. כִּי לוֹ יָאֶה.

דָּגוּל בִּמְלוּכָה.	עָנָיו בִּמְלוּכָה.
הָדוּר כַּהֲלָכָה.	פּוֹדֶה כַּהֲלָכָה.
וָתִיקָיו יֹאמְרוּ לוֹ.	צַדִּיקָיו יֹאמְרוּ לוֹ.
לְךָ וּלְךָ. לְךָ כִּי לְךָ.	לְךָ וּלְךָ. לְךָ כִּי לְךָ.
לְךָ אַף לְךָ. לְךָ יְיָ הַמַּמְלָכָה.	לְךָ אַף לְךָ. לְךָ יְיָ הַמַּמְלָכָה.
כִּי לוֹ נָאֶה. כִּי לוֹ יָאֶה.	כִּי לוֹ נָאֶה. כִּי לוֹ יָאֶה.

זַכַּאי בִּמְלוּכָה.	קָדוֹשׁ בִּמְלוּכָה.
חָסִין כַּהֲלָכָה.	רַחוּם כַּהֲלָכָה.
טַפְסְרָיו יֹאמְרוּ לוֹ.	שִׁנְאַנָּיו יֹאמְרוּ לוֹ.
לְךָ וּלְךָ. לְךָ כִּי לְךָ.	לְךָ וּלְךָ. לְךָ כִּי לְךָ.
לְךָ אַף לְךָ. לְךָ יְיָ הַמַּמְלָכָה.	לְךָ אַף לְךָ. לְךָ יְיָ הַמַּמְלָכָה.
כִּי לוֹ נָאֶה. כִּי לוֹ יָאֶה.	כִּי לוֹ נָאֶה. כִּי לוֹ יָאֶה.

יָחִיד בִּמְלוּכָה.	תַּקִּיף בִּמְלוּכָה.
כַּבִּיר כַּהֲלָכָה.	תּוֹמֵךְ כַּהֲלָכָה.
לִמּוּדָיו יֹאמְרוּ לוֹ.	תְּמִימָיו יֹאמְרוּ לוֹ.
לְךָ וּלְךָ. לְךָ כִּי לְךָ.	לְךָ וּלְךָ. לְךָ כִּי לְךָ.
לְךָ אַף לְךָ. לְךָ יְיָ הַמַּמְלָכָה.	לְךָ אַף לְךָ. לְךָ יְיָ הַמַּמְלָכָה.
כִּי לוֹ נָאֶה. כִּי לוֹ יָאֶה	כִּי לוֹ נָאֶה. כִּי לוֹ יָאֶה.

HALLEL

The Hallel is a series of psalms (113–118) which the Levites chanted during services in the Holy Temple in Jerusalem. This Hallel is sometimes called the Egyptian Hallel because of the reference to the exodus from Egypt.

The first two psalms (113–114) are recited before the meal.

The remainder of the psalms are recited after the Seder meal.

Why do we break up the Hallel into two sections? Because we wish to prolong the holiness of the Seder service. By sandwiching the meal between the two Hallels, the eating becomes a holy service.

יְיָ זְכָרָנוּ יְבָרֵךְ, Adonai remembers us with blessing

יְבָרֵךְ אֶת־בֵּית יִשְׂרָאֵל.	God will bless the House of Israel.
יְבָרֵךְ אֶת־בֵּית אַהֲרֹן.	God will bless the House of Aaron.
יְבָרֵךְ יִרְאֵי יְיָ,	Blessed are those who honor Adonai.
הַקְּטַנִּים עִם־הַגְּדֹלִים.	the young and the old alike.
יֹסֵף יְיָ עֲלֵיכֶם,	May Adonai send many blessings,
עֲלֵיכֶם וְעַל־בְּנֵיכֶם.	For you and your children.
בְּרוּכִים אַתֶּם לַיְיָ,	May you be blessed by Adonai,
עֹשֵׂה שָׁמַיִם וָאָרֶץ.	Creator of heaven and earth:
הַשָּׁמַיִם שָׁמַיִם לַיְיָ,	The heavens belong to Adonai,
וְהָאָרֶץ נָתַן לִבְנֵי־אָדָם.	The earth belongs to humans.
לֹא־הַמֵּתִים יְהַלְלוּ־יָהּ,	The dead cannot sing Halleluyah,
וְלֹא כָּל־יֹרְדֵי דוּמָה׃	Those who keep silent cannot praise God.
וַאֲנַחְנוּ נְבָרֵךְ יָהּ,	But we will bless the Lord forever.
מֵעַתָּה וְעַד־עוֹלָם הַלְלוּיָהּ.	Halleluyah—Praise the Lord.

הוֹדוּ לַיְיָ כִּי־טוֹב. Give thanks, for Adonai is good.

כִּי לְעוֹלָם חַסְדּוֹ.	God's mercy is forever.
יֹאמַר־נָא יִשְׂרָאֵל.	Let Israel say,
כִּי לְעוֹלָם חַסְדּוֹ.	God's mercy is forever.
יֹאמְרוּ־נָא בֵית־אַהֲרֹן.	Let the House of Aaron say
כִּי לְעוֹלָם חַסְדּוֹ.	God's mercy is forever.
יֹאמְרוּ־נָא יִרְאֵי יְיָ.	Let those who love Adonai say,
כִּי לְעוֹלָם חַסְדּוֹ.	God's mercy is forever.

ELIJAH THE PROPHET

In the center of the table is a large cup of wine. This cup of wine is for Elijah the Prophet.

Elijah lived thousands of years ago. The Bible tells us that he performed many miracles.

We believe that someday Elijah will return to earth. When he comes, then the whole world will live in peace and in freedom.

During the Seder, we open the door for Elijah the Prophet.

Fill the fourth cup of wine and open the door for Elijah the Prophet. All rise.

שְׁפֹךְ חֲמָתְךָ   Pour out Your anger

אֶל־הַגּוֹיִם אֲשֶׁר לֹא־יְדָעוּךָ,	upon the nations that do not know You,
וְעַל־מַמְלָכוֹת	and upon the kingdoms
אֲשֶׁר בְּשִׁמְךָ לֹא קָרָאוּ:	that do not recognize Your name:
כִּי אָכַל אֶת־יַעֲקֹב.	for they have destroyed Jacob
וְאֶת־נָוֵהוּ הֵשַׁמּוּ:	and ruined the land.
שְׁפָךְ־עֲלֵיהֶם זַעְמֶךָ,	Pour out Your anger upon them,
וַחֲרוֹן אַפְּךָ יַשִּׂיגֵם.	and let Your rage reach them.
תִּרְדֹּף בְּאַף	Chase them in anger,
וְתַשְׁמִידֵם,	and destroy them.
מִתַּחַת שְׁמֵי יְיָ.	From under the heavens of Adonai.

Open your door and recite the prayer, Sh'foch Hamatcha to show that you are free and unafraid, that you and your family are celebrating Passover for all the world to see and to witness.

We end the seder with a wish for peace

נַעַר הָיִיתִי גַּם זָקַנְתִּי	Once I was young, and now I am aged.
וְלֹא רָאִיתִי	in my lifetime I have never seen
צַדִּיק נֶעֱזָב	a good person forsaken,
וְזַרְעוֹ מְבַקֶּשׁ־לָחֶם:	or children begging for a living.
יְיָ עֹז לְעַמּוֹ יִתֵּן,	Adonai will give us strength,
יְיָ יְבָרֵךְ אֶת־עַמּוֹ בַשָּׁלוֹם.	Adonai will bless us with peace.

ANI MA'AMIN

In some homes a new ceremony has been introduced before opening the door for Elijah the Prophet. During the ceremony we remember the six million Jews who were murdered by the Nazis and the heroes of the ghetto revolts.

We sing the song **Ani Ma'amin.** This Song of Hope was sung by the martyrs in the concentration camps.

The words were written in accordance with the teachings of the famous Jewish philosopher, Moses Maimonides.

אֲנִי מַאֲמִין	I believe
אֲנִי מַאֲמִין, אֲנִי מַאֲמִין	I believe, I believe
בֶּאֱמוּנָה שְׁלֵמָה, בֶּאֱמוּנָה שְׁלֵמָה	with all my faith, with all my faith
בְּבִיאַת הַמָּשִׁיחַ,	that the Messiah will come,
בְּבִיאַת הַמָּשִׁיחַ	that the Messiah will come
אֲנִי מַאֲמִין.	I believe.

THE THIRD CUP OF WINE

We recite the blessing and drink the third of the four cups of wine. This cup recalls God's third promise, "I will redeem you."

Recite the blessing and drink the third cup of wine.

בָּרוּךְ אַתָּה יְיָ, Blessed is Adonai
אֱלֹהֵינוּ מֶלֶךְ הָעוֹלָם, our God ruler of the world
בּוֹרֵא פְּרִי הַגָּפֶן. who created the fruit of the vine.

Leader:
בָּרוּךְ הוּא **Blessed be Adonai**

וּבָרוּךְ שְׁמוֹ.	and blessed be the holy name.
בָּרוּךְ אַתָּה יְיָ,	Blessed is Adonai, our God.
אֱלֹהֵינוּ מֶלֶךְ הָעוֹלָם,	Ruler of the world
הַזָּן אֶת־הָעוֹלָם כֻּלּוֹ,	who nourishes the whole world
בְּטוּבוֹ, בְּחֵן בְּחֶסֶד וּבְרַחֲמִים,	with goodness, grace, and mercy.
הוּא נוֹתֵן לֶחֶם לְכָל־בָּשָׂר,	God gives food to all,
כִּי לְעוֹלָם חַסְדּוֹ.	God's mercy is forever.
וּבְטוּבוֹ הַגָּדוֹל,	God's goodness
תָּמִיד לֹא־חָסַר לָנוּ,	has never failed us, with food
וְאַל־יֶחְסַר לָנוּ מָזוֹן	and will never fail us
לְעוֹלָם וָעֶד.	forever and ever,
בַּעֲבוּר שְׁמוֹ הַגָּדוֹל,	for the sake of God's great name.
כִּי הוּא אֵל זָן וּמְפַרְנֵס לַכֹּל	God provides for all,
וּמֵטִיב לַכֹּל	helps all, and supports all,
וּמֵכִין מָזוֹן	preparing food
לְכָל־בְּרִיּוֹתָיו אֲשֶׁר בָּרָא.	for all the creatures God created.
בָּרוּךְ אַתָּה יְיָ,	Blessed is Adonai
הַזָּן אֶת־הַכֹּל.	who provides food for all.

וּבְנֵה יְרוּשָׁלַיִם **Build Jerusalem**

עִיר הַקֹּדֶשׁ, בִּמְהֵרָה בְיָמֵינוּ.	our Holy City, speedily in our time.
בָּרוּךְ אַתָּה יְיָ,	Blessed is Adonai,
בּוֹנֶה בְרַחֲמָיו יְרוּשָׁלָיִם.	who in mercy rebuilds Jerusalem.
אָמֵן.	Amen.

Why do we Jews love Israel and Jerusalem?

Because the greatest things that ever happened in Jewish history took place in Jerusalem. King Solomon built the Holy Temple in Jerusalem. Great Jewish kings ruled in Jerusalem. Many miracles happened in Jerusalem. Three times a year, on Sukkot, Pesach, and Shavuot, Jewish farmers brought sacrifices to the Holy Temple in Jerusalem.

So holy is Jerusalem that we recite our prayers facing Jerusalem, to our east.

בָּרֵךְ
BARECH
Thanks

The twelfth ceremony of the Seder is known as Barech. After the Afikomen the Seder resumes with the "thank you" prayer, Birkat Hamazon.

BIRKAT HAMAZON

The Seder meal is finished and we recite a special "thank you" prayer called "Birkat Hamazon." When we say the Birkat Hamazon we are thanking God for the food that we have eaten. We ask God to keep on blessing our parents, our relatives, our friends, and the whole world, with food and with peace.

Why do we say the Birkat Hamazon after we eat? Because the Birkat Hamazon is our way of saying "thank you" for God's delicious life-giving food. Fruits and vegetables grow from tiny seeds. God created these tiny food factories and helps them grow into delicious food.

If you eat these foods, you will, grow into a strong healthy, person.

רַבּוֹתַי נְבָרֵךְ:	Leader:	Friends, let us give thanks:
יְהִי שֵׁם יְיָ מְבֹרָךְ מֵעַתָּה וְעַד עוֹלָם.	Friends:	May Adonai be blessed, now and forever.
בִּרְשׁוּת מָרָנָן וְרַבָּנָן וְרַבּוֹתַי, נְבָרֵךְ [אֱלֹהֵינוּ] שֶׁאָכַלְנוּ מִשֶּׁלּוֹ	Leader:	With your permission, my friends, let us praise the One whose food we have eaten.
בָּרוּךְ [אֱלֹהֵינוּ] שֶׁאָכַלְנוּ מִשֶּׁלּוֹ וּבְטוּבוֹ חָיִינוּ.	Friends:	Blessed is the One whose food we have eaten and by whose goodness we live.

Our Rabbis say that the person who recites Grace with true thankfulness will never go hungry.

צָפוּן
TZAFUN
Afikomen

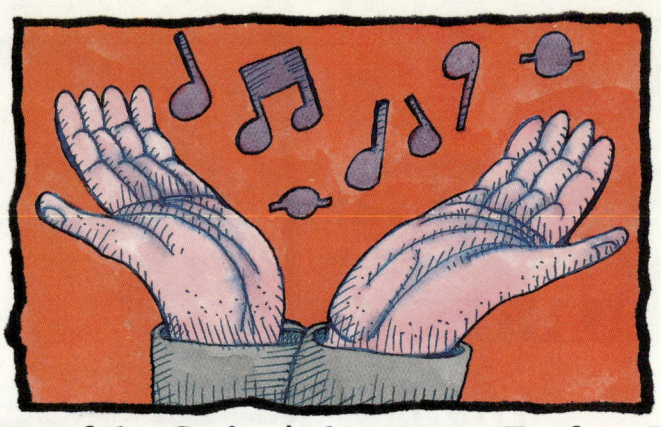

The eleventh ceremony of the Seder is known as Tzafun. The word Tzafun means "hidden."

At the end of the meal, the children search for the Afikomen which has been hidden by the Seder leader. The Seder cannot be completed without the Afikomen. So, whoever finds the Afikomen gets a reward.

Nothing is eaten after the Afikomen, so that matzah, the bread of freedom, is the last food tasted.

Why do we have an Afikomen at the Seder? Because when you are a slave nobody is kind to you and gives you presents. The Seder is your "freedom birthday party." And what's a birthday party without presents?

Some Sephardic Jews place the Afikomen on their shoulder for several moments to remind us that the Israelites carried the matzah dough on their shoulders when they were freed from Egypt.

SHULCHAN ORECH
שֻׁלְחָן עוֹרֵךְ
Mealtime

The tenth ceremony of the Seder is known as Shulchan Orech—mealtime.

In some places the meal begins with hard-boiled eggs dipped in salt water. The egg symbolizes new growth, new life, and hope.

The roasted egg on the Seder plate represents the Passover offering during Temple days.

Some scholars believe that the custom of eating a hard-boiled egg is based on the following idea: The more you boil an egg, the tougher it becomes. The more the Egyptians punished the Israelites, the stronger and tougher thay became.

כּוֹרֵךְ
KORECH
The Sandwich

The ninth step in the Seder ceremony is Korech—the sandwich. In this ceremony you make a sandwich of maror between two pieces of matzot. No blessing is recited.

Why do you make a sandwich of matzah and maror? Because matzah and maror together tell the story of Passover.

The lives of the Jews in Egypt were filled with maror. After the tenth plague they left Egypt in a great hurry. The raw dough had no time to rise and turn into bread. So our ancestors strapped the raw dough to their backpacks and let the hot desert sun bake the dough into matzot.

Eat a sandwich of bitter herbs and matzah while leaning on your left side. Use the third matzah.

זֵכֶר לְמִקְדָּשׁ כְּהִלֵּל. **In remembrance of the Holy Temple,**

כֵּן עָשָׂה הִלֵּל, We do as Hillel did
בִּזְמַן שֶׁבֵּית הַמִּקְדָּשׁ הָיָה קַיָּם. in Temple times:
הָיָה כּוֹרֵךְ מַצָּה וּמָרוֹר He put matzah and maror together,
וְאוֹכֵל בְּיַחַד. and ate them as a sandwich.
לְקַיֵּם מַה שֶׁנֶּאֱמַר: To observe the words of the Torah:
עַל־מַצּוֹת וּמְרֹרִים "They shall eat the Passover offering
יֹאכְלֻהוּ. with matzah and maror."

מָרוֹר
MAROR
Bitter Herbs

Point to the bitter herbs.

The eighth step in the Seder ceremony is called Maror—bitter herbs. In this ceremony we dip the maror into the haroset and recite a blessing.

Why do we eat maror at the Seder? Because Maror—bitter herbs—reminds us of the pain and suffering of our people in Egypt.

Why do we eat haroset at the Seder? Because the haroset reminds us of the cement our people made when they were slaves in Egypt.

Dip the maror into the haroset and recite the following blessing:

בָּרוּךְ אַתָּה יְיָ, **Blessed is Adonai,**
אֱלֹהֵינוּ מֶלֶךְ הָעוֹלָם, our God, ruler of the world,
אֲשֶׁר קִדְּשָׁנוּ בְּמִצְוֹתָיו, who made us holy by the mitzvot
וְצִוָּנוּ עַל־אֲכִילַת מָרוֹר. and commanded us to eat maror.

מוֹצִיא מַצָּה

MOTZI MATZAH

Eating Matzah

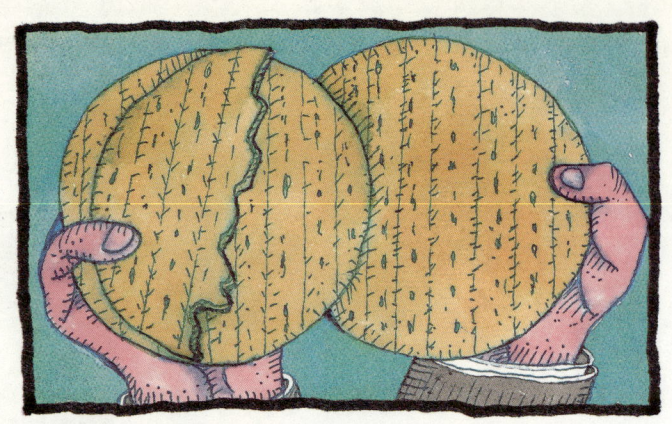

The seventh ceremony of the Seder is Motzi Matzah.
After the washing of the hands the leader recites two blessings over the three matzot. The leader gives two pieces of matzah to everyone at the Seder table. You eat the matzah leaning to the left side.

Say the two blessings over the matzah.

בָּרוּךְ אַתָּה יְיָ, **Blessed is Adonai,**
אֱלֹהֵינוּ מֶלֶךְ הָעוֹלָם, our God, ruler of the world,
הַמּוֹצִיא לֶחֶם מִן־הָאָרֶץ. who creates the bread from the earth.

Hold the piece of the middle matzah and say.

בָּרוּךְ אַתָּה יְיָ, **Blessed is Adonai,**
אֱלֹהֵינוּ מֶלֶךְ הָעוֹלָם, Our God, ruler of the world,
אֲשֶׁר קִדְּשָׁנוּ בְּמִצְוֹתָיו, who made us holy by the mitzvot
וְצִוָּנוּ עַל־אֲכִילַת מַצָּה: and commanded us to eat matzah.

Eat the piece of the upper and middle matzah while leaning on your left side.

THE SECOND CUP OF WINE

We recite the blessing and drink the second of the four cups of wine. This cup recalls God's second promise, "I will deliver you from bondage."

Recite the blessing and drink the second cup of wine. Drink the wine leaning on your left side.

בָּרוּךְ אַתָּה יְיָ, **Blessed is Adonai**
אֱלֹהֵינוּ מֶלֶךְ הָעוֹלָם, Our God ruler of the world
בּוֹרֵא, פְּרִי הַגָּפֶן. who created the fruit of the vine.

רַחְצָה
RACHTZAH
Washing

The sixth ceremony of the Seder is called Rachtzah—the washing of the hands.

As before every meal, you wash your hands and recite the blessing.

Wash your hands and say:

בָּרוּךְ אַתָּה יְיָ, **Blessed is Adonai,**
אֱלֹהֵינוּ מֶלֶךְ הָעוֹלָם, our God, ruler of the world,
אֲשֶׁר קִדְּשָׁנוּ בְּמִצְוֹתָיו, who has made us holy with mitzvot,
וְצִוָּנוּ עַל־נְטִילַת יָדָיִם. and commanded us to wash our hands.

Raise the wine cup and say.

Blessed is Adonai,
בָּרוּךְ אַתָּה יְיָ,

our God, ruler of the world,
אֱלֹהֵינוּ מֶלֶךְ הָעוֹלָם,

who has freed us,
אֲשֶׁר גְּאָלָנוּ

and freed our ancestors from Egypt,
וְגָאַל אֶת־אֲבוֹתֵינוּ מִמִּצְרָיִם,

who brought us to this night,
וְהִגִּיעָנוּ הַלַּיְלָה הַזֶּה,

on which we eat matzah
לֶאֱכָל־בּוֹ מַצָּה

and maror.
וּמָרוֹר.

Adonai, our God
כֵּן, יְיָ אֱלֹהֵינוּ

and God of our ancestors,
וֵאלֹהֵי אֲבוֹתֵינוּ,

help us to celebrate Holy Days and Festivals
יַגִּיעֵנוּ לְמוֹעֲדִים וְלִרְגָלִים אֲחֵרִים,

in peace,
הַבָּאִים לִקְרָאתֵנוּ לְשָׁלוֹם,

joyful in the rebuilding of Your city
שְׂמֵחִים בְּבִנְיַן עִירֶךָ,

And joyful in Your service,
וְשָׂשִׂים בַּעֲבוֹדָתֶךָ,

and there we will share in the Passover offerings.
וְנֹאכַל שָׁם מִן הַזְּבָחִים וּמִן הַפְּסָחִים,

We will sing a new song of thanks,
וְנוֹדֶה לְךָ שִׁיר חָדָשׁ עַל־גְּאֻלָּתֵנוּ

for our freedom,
וְעַל־פְּדוּת נַפְשֵׁנוּ.

Blessed are you, Adonai,
בָּרוּךְ אַתָּה יְיָ,

redeemer of Israel.
גָּאַל יִשְׂרָאֵל.

Halleluyah!

הַלְלוּיָהּ.

הַלְלוּ Give praise,

עַבְדֵי יְיָ. servants of Adonai,

הַלְלוּ אֶת־שֵׁם יְיָ: Praise the name of Adonai:

יְהִי שֵׁם יְיָ מְבֹרָךְ. Blessed be Adonai

מֵעַתָּה וְעַד־עוֹלָם: From now and forever.

מִמִּזְרַח־שֶׁמֶשׁ עַד־מְבוֹאוֹ. From rising sun to setting sun.

מְהֻלָּל שֵׁם יְיָ Praise Adonai,

הַלְלוּיָהּ. Halleluyah

בְּצֵאת יִשְׂרָאֵל מִמִּצְרַיִם, When Israel left Egypt,

בֵּית יַעֲקֹב the House of Jacob left people of a

מֵעַם לֹעֵז: strange language;

הָיְתָה יְהוּדָה לְקָדְשׁוֹ. Judah became a holy place

יִשְׂרָאֵל מַמְשְׁלוֹתָיו. Israel became God's Kingdom.

הַיָּם רָאָה וַיָּנֹס. הַיַּרְדֵּן יִסֹּב לְאָחוֹר. The sea fled, the Jordan retreated.

הֶהָרִים רָקְדוּ כְאֵילִים. Mountains leaped like rams,

גְּבָעוֹת כִּבְנֵי־צֹאן. hills skipped like lambs.

מַה־לְּךָ הַיָּם כִּי תָנוּס. Oh sea, why do you flee?

הַיַּרְדֵּן תִּסֹּב לְאָחוֹר. Jordan, why do you retreat?

הֶהָרִים תִּרְקְדוּ כְאֵילִים. Mountains, why leap like rams?

גְּבָעוֹת כִּבְנֵי־צֹאן. Hills, why skip like lambs?

מִלִּפְנֵי אָדוֹן Before the Lord,

חוּלִי אָרֶץ. even the earth shook at the

מִלִּפְנֵי אֱלוֹהַּ יַעֲקֹב. before the presence of Jacob's God.

הַהֹפְכִי הַצּוּר אֲגַם־מָיִם. Who turns rocks into pools of water.

חַלָּמִישׁ לְמַעְיְנוֹ־מָיִם. And flint into fountains.

Moses bowed down and asked God to help them.

"Stretch out your rod over the water," said God. Lo and behold! When Moses stretched his rod over the Red Sea, the waters parted and left a path of dry land. With a joyful shout, Moses led the Children of Israel across to the other side.

When the Egyptians saw them marching into the sea, they followed with their chariots and their horses. But the sand was no longer hard; it had become soft, and their chariot wheels were caught in it. Many wheels broke off the chariots. And the horses sank in the mud and fell down, so that the army was in confusion, and all were frightened.

By this time, all the Israelites had passed through the Red Sea and were standing on the high ground beyond it, looking at their enemies slowly struggling through the sand, all in one heaped-up mass of men and horses and chariots. Then Moses lifted up his hand, and at once a great tide of water swept up from the sea on the south. The road over which the Israelites had walked in safety was now covered with water. And the host of Pharaoh, with all his chariots and his horses and their riders, were drowned in the sea, before the eyes of the people of Israel.

Safe on the other side, Moses and the Children of Israel bent their heads and thanked God for helping them.

Because of God's miracles in Egypt we celebrate the holiday of Passover.

The Jews of Egypt were faced with a choice. Slavery in a civilized country with houses and marketplaces or freedom in a hot, sandy, hostile desert.

The Israelites placed their faith in God and left Egypt with no food—just matzah and the clothing they carried on their backs.

Were they marching into a deathtrap or into freedom? They believed in the power of the Almighty, and their march was a journey of trust and faith.

On Passover each of us is obligated to picture ourselves as if we lived in Egypt. Each of us is obligated to feel the bitterness of slavery and the joy of freedom.

CROSSING THE RED SEA

Suddenly, early in the morning, the Israelites went out of the land after more than 200 years in Egypt. They went out in order, like a great army, family by family and tribe by tribe, after joyfully gathering everything they owned, even the bread which had been started that evening, but which didn't have time to rise. Because the Children of Israel took that flat, unleavened bread (matzah) with them out of Egypt, unleavened bread is still eaten at Passover time, in memory of that day when Moses led his people out of slavery. Marching ahead of them was their great leader, Moses. And God sent a pillar of cloud to lead them by day, and a pillar of fire by night.

But back in the land of Egypt, Pharaoh was wishing he had not let the Hebrews go. For now the Egyptians had to do all the hard work. Pharaoh called one of his captains to him and said:

"Which way did the Hebrews go?"

"They are marching toward the Red Sea," said the captain.

"They will never be able to cross it," said Pharaoh. "Send an army after the Hebrews at once. We must have our slaves back again!"

Tramp, tramp, tramp, marched the Children of Israel.

Gallop-a-gallop-a-gallop came the Egyptian army behind them.

When the Hebrews reached the Red Sea, they heard the sound of galloping horses.

"The Egyptians!" cried the Children of Israel. "They have come after us!"

Then they cried to Moses:

"You have led us into the wilderness to be killed like dogs!"

Suddenly, Pharaoh and his ministers saw the land of Egypt without the Israelites. They saw empty brickyards and the construction of pyramids and palaces at a standstill. After several emergency meetings, the decision was made to chase after the Israelites and bring them back.

Point to the Bitter Herbs.

מָרוֹר זֶה ## These bitter herbs

שֶׁאָנוּ אוֹכְלִים, — which we eat,
עַל־שׁוּם מָה? — What is the reason for it?
עַל־שׁוּם, שֶׁמֵּרְרוּ הַמִּצְרִים — Because the Egyptians embittered
אֶת־חַיֵּי אֲבוֹתֵינוּ בְּמִצְרַיִם. — the lives of our ancestors in Egypt.

בְּכָל־דּוֹר וָדוֹר ## In every generation

חַיָּב אָדָם לִרְאוֹת אֶת־עַצְמוֹ, — it is our duty to see ourselves
כְּאִלּוּ הוּא יָצָא מִמִּצְרָיִם. — as coming out of Egypt.

לְפִיכָךְ, ## Therefore

אֲנַחְנוּ חַיָּבִים לְהוֹדוֹת, — it is our duty to thank,
לְהַלֵּל, — to praise,
לְשַׁבֵּחַ, לְפָאֵר, לְרוֹמֵם, לְהַדֵּר, — to pay tribute, to glorify, to exalt,
לְבָרֵךְ, לְעַלֵּה וּלְקַלֵּס, — to bless, to esteem, and to honor
לְמִי שֶׁעָשָׂה — the one who performed miracles
לַאֲבוֹתֵינוּ וְלָנוּ, — for our ancestors,
אֶת־כָּל־הַנִּסִּים הָאֵלֶּה. — and for us.
הוֹצִיאָנוּ מֵעַבְדוּת לְחֵרוּת. — God brought us from slavery to to freedom,
מִיָּגוֹן לְשִׂמְחָה. — from sadness to joy,
וּמֵאֵבֶל לְיוֹם טוֹב. — from sadness to happy holidays,
וּמֵאֲפֵלָה לְאוֹר גָּדוֹל. — from darkness to light,
וּמִשִּׁעְבּוּד לִגְאֻלָּה. — and from slavery to freedom.
וְנֹאמַר לְפָנָיו שִׁירָה חֲדָשָׁה, — Let us sing a new song, to God,

הַלְלוּיָהּ. ## Halleluyah!

The word Halleluyah is a combination of two Hebrew words: *Hallelu*, הַלְלוּ "give praise to," and *yah*, יָהּ "God": give praise to God

רַבָּן גַּמְלִיאֵל Rabban Gamliel

הָיָה אוֹמֵר: used to say:
כָּל־שֶׁלֹּא־אָמַר "Whoever does not explain
שְׁלֹשָׁה דְבָרִים אֵלוּ בַּפֶּסַח the meaning of these three Passover symbols
לֹא־יָצָא יְדֵי חוֹבָתוֹ. וְאֵלּוּ הֵן. has not fulfilled the purpose of the Seder.

פֶּסַח THE PASSOVER OFFERING
מַצָּה THE MATZAH
וּמָרוֹר THE BITTER HERBS

Point to the Shankbone.

פֶּסַח This Passover offering

שֶׁהָיוּ אֲבוֹתֵינוּ אוֹכְלִים, which our ancestors ate
בִּזְמַן שֶׁבֵּית־הַמִּקְדָּשׁ הָיָה קַיָּם, in Temple days,
עַל־שׁוּם מָה? what was the reason for it?
עַל־שׁוּם, Because
שֶׁפָּסַח הַקָּדוֹשׁ בָּרוּךְ הוּא, the Holy One "passed over"
עַל־בָּתֵּי אֲבוֹתֵינוּ בְּמִצְרָיִם. the houses of our ancestors in Egypt.

Point to the Matzah.

מַצָּה זוֹ This matzah

שֶׁאָנוּ אוֹכְלִים which we eat,
עַל־שׁוּם מָה? what is the reason for it?
עַל־שׁוּם, שֶׁלֹּא הִסְפִּיק בְּצֵקָם Because there was not enough time
שֶׁל אֲבוֹתֵינוּ לְהַחֲמִיץ, for the dough of our ancestors to become leavened
עַד שֶׁנִּגְלָה עֲלֵיהֶם, before the ruler of all,
מֶלֶךְ מַלְכֵי הַמְּלָכִים, the Holy One, revealed Himself,
הַקָּדוֹשׁ בָּרוּךְ הוּא, וּגְאָלָם: and freed them.

The Israelite families who sprinkled the blood of the lamb on their doorposts placed their lives in danger.

The lamb was one of the sacred gods of Egypt. Any Israelite caught sacrificing a lamb would most certainly be killed. The Israelites, who believed in God, performed the sacrifice and God saved them from the Egyptians.

אִלּוּ סִפֵּק צָרְכֵּנוּ בַּמִּדְבָּר אַרְבָּעִים שָׁנָה,
וְלֹא־הֶאֱכִילָנוּ אֶת־הַמָּן, דַּיֵּנוּ.
אִלּוּ הֶאֱכִילָנוּ אֶת־הַמָּן,
וְלֹא־נָתַן לָנוּ אֶת־הַשַּׁבָּת, דַּיֵּנוּ.
אִלּוּ נָתַן לָנוּ אֶת־הַשַּׁבָּת,
וְלֹא קֵרְבָנוּ לִפְנֵי הַר־סִינַי,
דַּיֵּנוּ.
אִלּוּ קֵרְבָנוּ לִפְנֵי הַר־סִינַי,
וְלֹא־נָתַן לָנוּ אֶת־הַתּוֹרָה, דַּיֵּנוּ.
אִלּוּ נָתַן לָנוּ אֶת־הַתּוֹרָה,
וְלֹא־הִכְנִיסָנוּ לְאֶרֶץ יִשְׂרָאֵל, דַּיֵּנוּ.
אִלּוּ הִכְנִיסָנוּ לְאֶרֶץ יִשְׂרָאֵל,
וְלֹא־בָנָה לָנוּ אֶת־בֵּית הַבְּחִירָה,
דַּיֵּנוּ.

If God had helped us for forty years in the desert
without feeding us manna, Dayenu!
If God had fed us manna,
without giving us the Shabbat, Dayenu!
If God had given us the Shabbat
without bringing us to Mount Sinai, Dayenu!
If God had brought us to Mount Sinai
without giving us the Torah, Dayenu!
If God had given us the Torah
us to the land of Israel, Dayenu!
If God had brought us to the land of Israel
without building the Holy Temple, Dayenu!
It would have been enough for us!

עַל אַחַת כַּמָּה וְכַמָּה טוֹבָה כְפוּלָה וּמְכֻפֶּלֶת לַמָּקוֹם עָלֵינוּ.

We are thankful to God for the many blessings given to us.

51

DAYENU

This is a song that retells the great deeds and miracles God performed for the Israelites. Each line ends with the word *Dayenu*—"it would have been enough for us."

כַּמָּה מַעֲלוֹת טוֹבוֹת לַמָּקוֹם עָלֵינוּ.	**We are thankful to God** for the good things done for us.
אִלּוּ הוֹצִיאָנוּ מִמִּצְרַיִם, וְלֹא־עָשָׂה בָהֶם שְׁפָטִים, דַּיֵּנוּ.	If God had brought us out from Egypt without judging the Egyptians, Dayenu! It would have been enough for us!
אִלּוּ עָשָׂה בָהֶם שְׁפָטִים, וְלֹא־עָשָׂה בֵאלֹהֵיהֶם, דַּיֵּנוּ.	If God had judged the Egyptians without destroying their idols, Dayenu.
אִלּוּ עָשָׂה בֵאלֹהֵיהֶם, וְלֹא־הָרַג אֶת־בְּכוֹרֵיהֶם, דַּיֵּנוּ.	If God had destroyed their idols without slaying their firstborn, Dayenu!
אִלּוּ הָרַג אֶת־בְּכוֹרֵיהֶם, וְלֹא־נָתַן לָנוּ אֶת־מָמוֹנָם, דַּיֵּנוּ.	If God had slain their firstborn without giving us their treasure, Dayenu!
אִלּוּ נָתַן לָנוּ אֶת־מָמוֹנָם, וְלֹא־קָרַע לָנוּ אֶת־הַיָּם, דַּיֵּנוּ.	If God had given us their treasure without splitting the sea for us, Dayenu!
אִלּוּ קָרַע לָנוּ אֶת־הַיָּם, וְלֹא־הֶעֱבִירָנוּ בְתוֹכוֹ בֶּחָרָבָה, דַּיֵּנוּ	If God had split the sea for us without leading us to dry land, Dayenu!
אִלּוּ הֶעֱבִירָנוּ בְתוֹכוֹ בֶּחָרָבָה, וְלֹא־שִׁקַּע צָרֵינוּ בְּתוֹכוֹ, דַּיֵּנוּ:	If God had brought us to dry land without drowning our enemies, Dayenu!
אִלּוּ שִׁקַּע צָרֵינוּ בְּתוֹכוֹ, וְלֹא־סִפֵּק צָרְכֵּנוּ בַּמִּדְבָּר אַרְבָּעִים שָׁנָה, דַּיֵּנוּ.	If God had drowned our enemies without helping us for forty years in the desert, Dayenu!

The Israelites left Egypt with much gold and silver. The Jews earned this treasure. The gold and silver was in payment for the many years they worked as slaves without payment.

Each person at the Seder spills out a drop of wine from their wine cup at the mention of each of the plagues. Some say that the drops of wine are tears of regret that freedom had to be purchased through the death of Egyptians.

1. BLOOD— דָם.
2. FROGS— צְפַרְדֵּעַ.
3. LICE— כִּנִּים.
4. FLIES— עָרוֹב.
5. CATTLE DISEASE— דֶּבֶר.
6. BOILS— שְׁחִין.
7. HAIL— בָּרָד.
8. LOCUSTS— אַרְבֶּה.
9. DARKNESS— חֹשֶׁךְ.
10. SLAYING OF THE FIRSTBORN— מַכַּת בְּכֹרוֹת:

Rabbi Judah was a wise and gentle man. He couldn't bring himself to recite the plagues. The rabbi felt that even though the Egyptians were enemies they were still God's creations. It pained him to recite the plagues. So Rabbi Judah formed the first letters of each plague into these three-word combinations;

D'ZACH, ADASH, B'A-CHAV.
דְּצַ"ךְ עֲדַ"שׁ בְּאַחַ"ב.

Why did God choose to punish the Egyptians with plagues? Because the plagues were God's revenge for the cruelty of the Egyptians against the Jews.

Because the Jews were forced to carry water for the Egyptians, the water turned into blood.

Because the Egyptians forced the Jews to catch fish for them, the rivers were filled with frogs.

Because the Egyptians murdered the male children of the Jews, God sent the tenth plague, which killed the young Egyptian boys.

"Tell your God to take them away!" cried Pharaoh. "I will let the Hebrews go!"

The frogs died, but Pharaoh did not keep his promise.

Then God sent millions of lice to bite the Egyptians. Even the great Pharaoh scratched and scratched until he could bear it no longer.

"Tell your God to take away the lice!" he cried. But when the lice were gone, Pharaoh still said, "No!"

Then came the flies. Then a terrible sickness that killed all the cattle. Then the bodies of the Egyptians broke out with boils. They itched all over and spent their days scratching themselves. Hail came and spoiled the crops. Locusts ate up what was left of the crops. Then came a terrible darkness that lasted for three days. But still Pharaoh would not let the Hebrews go.

"Let the firstborn of every Egyptian die!" said God.

Then came a time of weeping and sadness, for the firstborn son of every Egyptian family lay dead. Pharaoh's head was bowed with grief, for he, too, had lost his firstborn son.

"Take your flocks and your people," he cried to Moses, "and go from the land of Egypt."

Pharaoh had learned at last that the power of God is greater than the power of the greatest king.

With the coming of the tenth plague, the death of the firstborn children, Pharaoh finally surrendered. He begged Moses and Aaron to get the Israelites out of Egypt.

THE TEN PLAGUES

"How shall I help my people, O Lord," prayed Moses. "The Pharaoh is making them work harder than ever!"

"Ask Pharaoh again to set your people free," said God. "If he refused, then stretch out your rod over the river and the Egyptians will know I am the Lord!"

The next day, Pharaoh was standing beside the river Nile. Many of his people were gathered around him.

"My God commands that you set the Hebrews free," said Moses to Pharaoh.

"I told you I know nothing of your God!" cried Pharaoh.

"Then you shall know him!" said Moses.

He stretched his rod over the waters of the Nile. Suddenly, the Egyptians began screaming with fear. The waters of the great river had turned to blood! Every fish in the river was dead!

For seven days the Nile was a river of blood. The Egyptians were dying of thirst. Then the river became clear.

After this Moses spoke to Pharaoh.

"Now if you do not set my people free, the Lord will send thousands of frogs into your land."

But Pharaoh would not let the Hebrews go.

Then came the frogs.

The plagues were not brought upon the Egyptians without warning. Moses warned the Egyptians before some of the plagues. Moses hoped that the Egyptians would change their minds and allow the Israelites to leave. However, Pharaoh and his advisors just laughed at the warnings.

Pharaoh's eyes were cold and cruel.

"I know nothing of your God. Who is this God? Show me some of your God's wonders," said Pharaoh.

Aaron threw his rod upon the ground and it became a serpent.

"My magicians can do that much!" laughed Pharaoh. He called his magicians and told them to cast their rods upon the ground. The rods all turned into serpents. But quick as a wink, Aaron's rod ate up all the other rods.

Pharaoh became very angry.

"Get out of my sight!" he cried to Moses and Aaron. "And from this day on, the Hebrews will work harder than ever. They will not only make the bricks to build our storehouses—they will have to find the straw to put into the bricks!"

Moses and Aaron fled from the palace. Their hearts were heavy. Moses prayed.

"What have I done, O Lord?" he cried. "Now my people work harder than ever!"

"Do not fear, Moses," said God. "For I am with you always. The Egyptians will soon find out about the God of the Children of Israel!"

After the first meeting with Moses, the Pharaoh became very angry and decided to punish the Israelites. He ordered the taskmasters not to provide the straw for making bricks. In ancient Egypt mud bricks were the most important building materials. The straw made the bricks very strong. As punishment, Pharaoh insisted that the Israelites had to find their own straw but still produce the same amount of bricks.

MOSES TALKS TO PHARAOH

"Go into the wilderness and meet your brother Moses!"

These were the words God spoke to Aaron. Now Aaron stood on a mountaintop, waiting for his brother. In the distance, he saw a man walking. The man held his head high and in his hand he carried a rod.

"It is Moses, my brother," cried Aaron. When the brothers met, they kissed each other and wept, for they had not seen each other for many years.

Moses told Aaron about the many wonders God had shown him: the burning bush, and the rod that turned into a serpent then back into a rod again.

"Now we must go to Pharaoh," said Moses, "and ask him to set our people free."

"There is a new Pharaoh on the throne," said Aaron. "He is very cruel."

"Do not fear, my brother," said Moses. "God is with us."

When they reached Egypt, the brothers gathered together all the families of Israel, and Aaron told them that Moses had been chosen by God to lead them to their Promised Land.

Then Aaron and Moses went to see Pharaoh.

"The God of the Hebrews has sent us to lead the Children of Israel out of Egypt," said Aaron.

Why was Moses' rod so special that it is mentioned in the Haggadah? Because God gave the shepherd's rod special miracle-making abilities.

With the rod Moses helped bring the plagues. With the rod Moses split the Red Sea so the Israelites could escape.

Moses was puzzled, but he did as God told him. He threw his rod to the ground. The rod turned into a serpent! Moses turned and ran away from it.

But God called Moses and said:

"Do not be afraid! Put forth your hand and take the serpent by the tail!"

Moses fearfully obeyed. As his hand closed over the snake's tail it became a rod again in Moses' hand!

"Now go to Pharaoh and tell him you will lead the Hebrews out of Egypt," said God. "If the people do not believe you, show them these wonders."

"But they will not listen to me," pleaded Moses, "For I cannot speak well enough."

"Then your brother Aaron will speak for you," said God. "Now go into Egypt! And remember, I will be with you always."

Moses raised his head and looked at the bush. The flames were gone. Then Moses cried out:

"I am not afraid anymore, for God is with me. I shall lead my people out of Egypt and into their Promised Land!"

Then Moses began the journey back to Egypt. Little did he dream of the dangers before him, or the hardships he would have to overcome before the Children of Israel would find their Promised Land!

God chose to appear to Moses out of a simple, lowly thornbush. The bush, a very small tree, was chosen to indicate humility. The thorns were chosen to indicate readiness to identify with the sufferings of the Children of Israel.

THE BURNING BUSH

Far up on a hillside, a shepherd was watching his flock. The shepherd was Moses, and the sheep belonged to his father-in-law.

Moses had fled from Egypt into the land of Midian. There he had gone to live in the house of Jethro and had married one of Jethro's seven daughters, Zipporah.

But Moses still remembered that his people were slaves in the land of Egypt. As he watched the sheep on the lonely hillside, Moses thought:

"I wish I could do something to help my people."

"Baaaaa!" cried the sheep.

"That's strange," thought Moses. "The sheep seem to be afraid of something."

Then Moses saw a strange sight. Out of a large bush were coming great red flames. But the bush did not burn.

Suddenly, Moses began to tremble, for out of the flames came a voice.

"Moses!" cried the voice. "Take off your shoes, for you are standing upon holy ground!"

Moses took off his shoes and covered his face, for he knew this was the voice of God.

"Moses!" said God, "go and lead thy people out of the land of Egypt."

"I am afraid the people will not believe me when I tell them of this wonderful burning bush! How am I to make them believe that God spoke to me and chose me for their leader?"

"Moses!" commanded God. "Take your rod and throw it on the ground with all your strength!"

Moses and the Hebrew hid the dead Egyptian in the sand.

The next day, Moses saw two Hebrews fighting each other in the street.

"Don't you know it is wrong to fight together like that?" Moses cried.

But the men said to him:

"Who are you to tell us not to fight? You, who have killed an Egyptian! Are you going to kill us, too?"

When Moses heard this, he knew his secret had been found out.

"I must leave Egypt and hide in the wilderness," he thought. "For when the Pharaoh finds out I have killed an Egyptian, he will order his soldiers to kill me."

Before Moses left the land of Egypt, he went to say goodbye to Jocheved, his mother. Jocheved was an old woman now. Tears ran down her wrinkled cheeks as she kissed her son.

"Do not weep, mother," said Moses. "God will be with me wherever I go. And some day, God will set our people free."

The Egyptians tried, but could not break the spirit of the Hebrews. The Rabbis say that the Israelites never changed their Hebrew names to Egyptian ones. They continued speaking Hebrew and never informed on each other. The Hebrews also always married their own people.

These four things gave the Israelites strength to bear the pain of slavery.

MOSES FIGHTS FOR THE WEAK

In the palace of the Pharaoh of Egypt, there lived the young prince named Moses. But Moses was not a happy prince. The Pharaoh's daughter had treated him like her own son since the day she had found him in the bulrushes when he was a tiny baby. But Moses knew he was a Hebrew, and everywhere he went in the land of Egypt, he saw the Hebrews toiling as slaves.

One day, Moses saw some Hebrews hauling heavy stones along a road. Behind the Hebrews walked an Egyptian with a club. One of the Hebrews fell down in the road and could not go on.

"Get up, you lazy slave!" cried the Egyptian. Then he began to beat the Hebrew with his whip.

"Stop!" cried Moses. "Can't you see the poor man is too weak to move?"

But the Egyptian kept on beating the Hebrew. Moses became very angry. He struck the Egyptian so hard that the man fell to the ground dead.

"We must hide the body in the sand," cried the Hebrew. "If Pharaoh finds out you have killed an Egyptian, he will order your death!"

Moses was eager to see the condition of his Hebrew brothers. He was shocked to find one Hebrew abusing another and tried to make peace between them.

"Oh, what a beautiful little baby you are," she crooned to it, and when the baby reached up one of its fat little hands and tugged at her lovely long hair, the princess's eyes filled with tears. "It must be a Hebrew baby."

She was full of pity for the child.

The baby's sister Miriam had crept closer and closer, and she overheard the princess say these words. She ran forward and cried:

"Your Highness, I know where there is a Hebrew woman who can nurse this child. Shall I call her?"

"Yes, yes, have her come at once," cried the princess. And so little Miriam ran back to her home and told her mother about the wonderful thing that had happened. The mother was overjoyed. "God has answered my prayer," she cried.

The princess said to the mother:

"Take the child home and nurse him, and I shall pay you good wages for this service."

"I shall call the baby Moses," said the princess, "because this name means 'I drew him from the river.'"

The Nile is the longest river in Africa. It starts in the heart of Africa in Lake Victoria and flows nearly 3,000 miles into the Mediterranean Sea. The Nile provides the water which for thousands of years has flooded and fertilized Egypt. There have been times when a weak flow of water has led to widespread famine. It is quite likely that a shortage of rain led to the seven dry years in the days of Joseph.

THE EGYPTIAN PRINCESS

The daughter of the great Pharaoh of Egypt was walking beside the river Nile with her handmaidens.

"It is such a lovely day," said the princess; "let us walk along the river bank for a while before we go bathing."

Soon they came to a place where tall bulrushes grew beside the river.

"It is the daughter of the great Pharaoh," thought Miriam. "Oh dear, surely now my little baby brother will be found and killed!"

But Miriam was mistaken. For the Pharaoh's daughter was not like her father. She was as good and kind as she was beautiful. As she dipped her hands into the river, she saw something moving out on the water.

"Look," she cried to her handmaidens. "There is a little basket floating in the water." She sent one of her maids to bring it to her, so that she might see what was in the basket.

The handmaiden brought the basket to her mistress, and when the princess looked inside, the rosy face of a beautiful baby looked up at her, crying. Pharaoh's daughter's heart was softened, and she held the child close to her.

"Mother, mother!" they cried. "The king's soldiers are coming!"

Jochebed quickly hid the baby under a pile of clothing. Just then, the soldiers knocked on the door.

"Is there a baby boy in this house?" they cried.

"No!" answered Jochebed. "I have just two children, Miriam and Aaron."

But Jochebed knew she could not keep her baby hidden forever.

"I shall make a basket of reeds," she said to her husband. "You must patch it with pitch so it will float on the water. I will put our little son into the basket and take it to the river. Perhaps some kind Egyptian family will find our baby."

When Jochebed placed her son in the little basket, her tears fell like rain on his sweet baby face.

"Come," Jochebed said to Miriam, "we will hide the basket in the bulrushes, by the river. Then we will watch and see what happens."

Then the Hebrew mother kissed her son gently, and set the basket boat upon the water. As she watched it float away down the river, she prayed silently.

"Watch over my baby, God," she said. "Somehow, someway, let him grow to be a man."

She watched the little basket until it was out of sight, and then she went sadly back to her house.

The reeds, six feet in height, were cut into thin strips and glued together to form sheets. These could be treated with tar to make the sheets watertight. These reeds also had leaves which were used to make paper and mats.

Bulrushes can be woven to make a basket. Pitch made the basket waterproof. The pitch was used on the outside rather than on the inside so that the child would suffer no discomfort from its odor.

BIRTH OF MOSES

As long as Joseph lived, and for some time after, the people of Israel were treated kindly by the Egyptians, out of their love for Joseph, who had saved Egypt from suffering by famine. But after a long time, another Pharaoh began to rule over Egypt, who cared nothing for Joseph or Joseph's people. When he saw how the Hebrews were multiplying and prospering, he was afraid they would seize the throne one day and rule all Egypt. Now the Hebrews had no such thought at all. In fact, they were hoping that someday a great leader would come and lead them to the land that God had promised Abraham, Isaac, and Jacob. The cruel Pharaoh made the Hebrews work as slaves. They carried all the heavy stones that were used to build the Egyptian temples and palaces.

One day, the wicked Pharaoh gave an order to his soldiers:

"There are too many Hebrews in the land of Egypt," he said. "From this day on, you must take every Hebrew boy that is born and throw him into the river Nile to drown."

Soon after this, a baby boy was born. His mother was Jocheved, wife of Amram, who belonged to the Hebrew tribe of Levi. Amram and Jocheved had two other children, named Miriam and Aaron. When the new baby was born, Jocheved held him tenderly in her arms.

"How can I let my beautiful little son be thrown into the river?" she cried. "I will hide him so the king's soldiers cannot find him."

For three months, Jocheved kept her baby son hidden. But one day, Miriam and Aaron came running into the house.

Joseph saved Egypt from famine by building storehouses for food and grain. Three hundred years later the Egyptians repaid Joseph's wisdom by forcing the Jews to build the storehouse cities of Pithom and Ramses.

THE CHILDREN OF ISRAEL

The Torah tells the early history of the Jewish people. It describes how God commanded Abraham to leave his country and his father's house and go to the land of Canaan, where he would become the founder of a "great nation."

Abraham and his wife, Sarah, obeyed God's command and journeyed to Canaan. Their son was Isaac, who married Rebecca. Their grandson was Jacob; and it was Jacob who went down to Egypt.

Why did Jacob journey to Egypt? Because Joseph, his son, had become prime minister to Pharaoh, king of Egypt. Joseph had saved Egypt from a great famine, and the king rewarded him and made him prime minister. When the famine broke out in Canaan, Joseph asked his father and all his family to join him there. Then Joseph gave his father and his brothers land, as Pharaoh had commanded. And Jacob (Israel) and his family lived in the land of Goshen; and they grew in numbers and were very successful farmers and shepherds.

Joseph and all his brothers died. Now a new king came to power, who knew nothing about Joseph and his contributions to Egypt.

Joseph had served the Hyksos, or "Shepherd Kings." The Hyksos were friendly to the Hebrews and gave them the land of Goshen in which to live.

Throughout history, wherever Jews have lived, new Pharaohs have arisen to persecute the Jewish people.

Raise the wine cup and say:

This promise

וְהִיא שֶׁעָמְדָה
לַאֲבוֹתֵינוּ וְלָנוּ.
שֶׁלֹּא אֶחָד בִּלְבָד,
עָמַד עָלֵינוּ
לְכַלּוֹתֵנוּ.
אֶלָּא שֶׁבְּכָל דּוֹר וָדוֹר,
עוֹמְדִים עָלֵינוּ לְכַלּוֹתֵנוּ.
וְהַקָּדוֹשׁ בָּרוּךְ הוּא מַצִּילֵנוּ
מִיָּדָם.

was made to our ancestors
and is also for us.
More than once enemies
have tried to destroy us;
in every generation they rise
and seek our destruction
but God saves us from
their hands.

Put down the wine cup.

And Adonai heard our cries.

וַיִּשְׁמַע יְיָ אֶת־קוֹלֵנוּ.
כְּמָה שֶׁנֶּאֱמַר:
וַיִּשְׁמַע אֱלֹהִים אֶת־נַאֲקָתָם.
וַיִּזְכֹּר אֱלֹהִים אֶת־בְּרִיתוֹ,
אֶת־אַבְרָהָם, אֶת־יִצְחָק וְאֶת־יַעֲקֹב.

As it is written:
And God heard their suffering.
And God remembered the Covenant,
with Abraham, Isaac, and Jacob.

And Adonai brought us out of Egypt.

וַיּוֹצִאֵנוּ יְיָ מִמִּצְרַיִם,
בְּיָד חֲזָקָה, וּבִזְרֹעַ נְטוּיָה,
וּבְמֹרָא גָּדֹל.
וּבְאֹתוֹת וּבְמֹפְתִים.

with a strong hand and outstretched arm,
and with great terror,
and with signs and with wonders.

The Torah tells us that even Joseph, second only to the Pharaoh, knew that Egypt was only a temporary stop-over. Joseph requested that his bones be removed from Egypt and buried in the land of Israel.

Four hundred and thirty years later the Israelites carried Joseph's coffin out of Egypt.

At first מִתְּחִלָּה

Our ancestors prayed to idols.	עוֹבְדֵי כוֹכָבִים הָיוּ אֲבוֹתֵינוּ.
And now God has brought us close.	וְעַכְשָׁו קֵרְבָנוּ הַמָּקוֹם לַעֲבוֹדָתוֹ.
As it is written:	שֶׁנֶּאֱמַר:
"And Joshua said to the people:	וַיֹּאמֶר יְהוֹשֻׁעַ אֶל־כָּל־הָעָם.
Adonai, God of Israel says,	כֹּה אָמַר יְיָ אֱלֹהֵי יִשְׂרָאֵל,
Your ancestors lived beyond the Euphrates River,	בְּעֵבֶר הַנָּהָר יָשְׁבוּ אֲבוֹתֵיכֶם מֵעוֹלָם,
Terah, the father of Abraham,	תֶּרַח אֲבִי אַבְרָהָם
and the father of Nahor	וַאֲבִי נָחוֹר.
They prayed to idols.	וַיַּעַבְדוּ אֱלֹהִים אֲחֵרִים.
And I led your ancestor,	וָאֶקַּח אֶת־אֲבִיכֶם
Abraham beyond the river,	אֶת־אַבְרָהָם מֵעֵבֶר הַנָּהָר,
and I led him through the land of Canaan.	וָאוֹלֵךְ אוֹתוֹ בְּכָל־אֶרֶץ כְּנָעַן.
I increased his descendants,	וָאַרְבֶּה אֶת־זַרְעוֹ,
I gave him Isaac.	וָאֶתֵּן־לוֹ אֶת־יִצְחָק.
And to Isaac I gave Jacob and Esau.	וָאֶתֵּן לְיִצְחָק אֶת־יַעֲקֹב וְאֶת־עֵשָׂו.
To Esau I gave Mount Seir, as an inheritance.	וָאֶתֵּן לְעֵשָׂו אֶת־הַר שֵׂעִיר, לָרֶשֶׁת אוֹתוֹ.
But Jacob and his children went down to Egypt."	וְיַעֲקֹב וּבָנָיו יָרְדוּ מִצְרָיִם.

Blessed בָּרוּךְ

is God who keeps the promise to Israel.	שׁוֹמֵר הַבְטָחָתוֹ לְיִשְׂרָאֵל.
Blessed is God.	בָּרוּךְ הוּא.
Who foretold the end of slavery to our ancestor Abraham at the Covenant of Sacrifices.	שֶׁהַקָּדוֹשׁ בָּרוּךְ הוּא חִשַּׁב אֶת־הַקֵּץ לַעֲשׂוֹת, כְּמָה שֶׁאָמַר לְאַבְרָהָם אָבִינוּ בִּבְרִית בֵּין הַבְּתָרִים.

Because of the famine in Canaan, Jacob and his family went down to Egypt. They did not become citizens and lived separately in the land of Goshen. Their goal was to return and live in Canaan (Israel), the land that God had promised Abraham, Isaac, and Jacob.

Blessed is God
בָּרוּךְ הַמָּקוֹם בָּרוּךְ הוּא.

בָּרוּךְ שֶׁנָּתַן תּוֹרָה
לְעַמּוֹ יִשְׂרָאֵל.
בָּרוּךְ הוּא.

who gave the Torah
to Israel.
Blessed is God.

כְּנֶגֶד אַרְבָּעָה בָנִים דִּבְּרָה תוֹרָה.
The Torah speaks about four children:

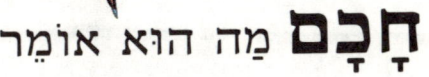

אֶחָד חָכָם,
וְאֶחָד רָשָׁע,
וְאֶחָד תָּם,
וְאֶחָד שֶׁאֵינוֹ יוֹדֵעַ לִשְׁאוֹל.

one who is wise,
and one who is bad,
one who is simple,
one who cannot ask a question.

חָכָם מַה הוּא אוֹמֵר
מָה הָעֵדֹת וְהַחֻקִּים
וְהַמִּשְׁפָּטִים,
אֲשֶׁר צִוָּה יְיָ אֱלֹהֵינוּ אֶתְכֶם.

The wise child asks:
"Please tell me the meaning of the rules, laws, customs which God has commanded us."

רָשָׁע מַה הוּא אוֹמֵר
מָה הָעֲבֹדָה הַזֹּאת לָכֶם.

The bad child asks:
"What is the meaning of this nonsense?"

תָּם מַה הוּא אוֹמֵר
מַה זֹּאת.

The simple child asks:
"What is all this?"

וְשֶׁאֵינוֹ יוֹדֵעַ לִשְׁאוֹל,
אַתְּ פְּתַח לוֹ.

The child who is not old enough to ask:
"You shall explain to them."

The four types of children need four different answers. Each person is special. Each person deserves an answer on his or her own level of understanding.

32

מַעֲשֶׂה בְּרַבִּי אֱלִיעֶזֶר
It is told that Rabbi Eliezer,

וְרַבִּי יְהוֹשֻׁעַ, וְרַבִּי אֶלְעָזָר בֶּן־עֲזַרְיָה,
וְרַבִּי עֲקִיבָא, וְרַבִּי טַרְפוֹן,
שֶׁהָיוּ מְסֻבִּין בִּבְנֵי־בְרָק,
וְהָיוּ מְסַפְּרִים
בִּיצִיאַת מִצְרַיִם, כָּל־אוֹתוֹ הַלַּיְלָה,
עַד שֶׁבָּאוּ תַלְמִידֵיהֶם
וְאָמְרוּ לָהֶם:
רַבּוֹתֵינוּ, הִגִּיעַ זְמַן קְרִיאַת
שְׁמַע, שֶׁל שַׁחֲרִית.

Rabbi Joshua, Rabbi Elazar the son of Azariah, Rabbi Akiba, and Rabbi Tarfon sat at the Seder in Bene-Berak, telling the story of the departure from Egypt, through the night. Towards morning their students came and said, "Our teachers, the time has come to recite the morning prayer of Sh'ma."

The story of the five rabbis points out the importance of telling and talking about the story of freedom. Even these five famous rabbis talked about and discussed the story of Passover.

The Seder ceremony helps us to understand the meaning of Passover. First we ask questions, and then we continue to the answers. The answer begins with Avadim Hayinu—"we were slaves."

Uncover the matzah and begin the answers.

THE ANSWERS

עֲבָדִים הָיִינוּ We were slaves

לְפַרְעֹה בְּמִצְרָיִם,	of Pharaoh in Egypt
וַיּוֹצִיאֵנוּ יְיָ אֱלֹהֵינוּ מִשָּׁם,	and God brought us out from there
בְּיָד חֲזָקָה	with a strong hand
וּבִזְרוֹעַ נְטוּיָה,	and an outstretched arm.
וְאִלּוּ לֹא הוֹצִיא, הַקָּדוֹשׁ בָּרוּךְ הוּא,	If God had not brought out
אֶת־אֲבוֹתֵינוּ מִמִּצְרָיִם,	our ancestors from Egypt
הֲרֵי אָנוּ, וּבָנֵינוּ,	then we, our children,
וּבְנֵי בָנֵינוּ,	and our children's children
מְשֻׁעְבָּדִים הָיִינוּ לְפַרְעֹה בְּמִצְרָיִם,	might still be in slavery in Egypt.
וַאֲפִלּוּ	Therefore, even if we were
כֻּלָּנוּ חֲכָמִים, כֻּלָּנוּ נְבוֹנִים,	all people of wisdom and understanding,
כֻּלָּנוּ זְקֵנִים,	and even if we were sages
כֻּלָּנוּ יוֹדְעִים אֶת־הַתּוֹרָה,	and Torah scholars,
מִצְוָה עָלֵינוּ לְסַפֵּר	it would still be a mitzvah to tell the story
בִּיצִיאַת מִצְרָיִם.	of the departure from Egypt.
וְכָל־הַמַּרְבֶּה לְסַפֵּר	The more a person tells of the
בִּיצִיאַת מִצְרָיִם	departure from Egypt,
הֲרֵי זֶה מְשֻׁבָּח.	the more is he or she to be praised.

The answer to the Four Questions starts with the Hebrew words *avadim hayinu*—"we were slaves."

THE FOUR QUESTIONS ARE ANSWERED IN ORDER

The following section is not part of the real Haggadah. It is included here as a direct reply to the Four Questions.

I. Q. **Why do we eat matzah?**
   A. Our ancestors left Egypt in a hurry. Their dough did not have time to rise.

II. Q. **Why do we eat bitter herbs?**
   A. We eat bitter herbs to remind us of the bitterness of slavery in Egypt.

III. Q. **Why do we dip twice?**
   A. The first time we dip karpas into salt water to show that we are now free people and can eat as we please. We use karpas because herbs are a sign of spring, and Passover is the holiday of the spring season.
   The second time we dip maror into haroset to show that the bitterness of Egypt has been sweetened. The maror represents the bitterness of life in Egypt. The haroset symbolizes the bricks our ancestors made in that land.

IV. Q. **Why do we recline at the table?**
   A. We recline as a sign of freedom and comfort.

In ancient times free people ate their meals in a leaning position, or stretched on couches. The leader conducts the Seder in a leaning position to show us that we are now *benai horin*, a free people.

THE FOUR QUESTIONS

Now it is question-and-answer time. The youngest person who is able asks the Arba Koosh-yot, the Four Questions.

Sometimes we call the Four Questions "Mah Nishtanah." These two Hebrew words are the first two words of the Four Questions.

Mah Nishtanah means "What is different?"

The answer to the Mah Nishtanah is the story of Passover. Why do we ask the Four Questions at the Passover Seder? Because only free people have the right to ask questions. Slaves cannot ask questions and must do exactly as they are told.

When you can ask as well as answer the Four Questions all by yourself, you can understand and feel the real meaning of Passover and of freedom.

מַה נִּשְׁתַּנָּה הַלַּיְלָה הַזֶּה, מִכָּל־הַלֵּילוֹת

What is different about this night from all other nights?

שֶׁבְּכָל הַלֵּילוֹת, אָנוּ אוֹכְלִין חָמֵץ וּמַצָּה, הַלַּיְלָה הַזֶּה כֻּלּוֹ מַצָּה.

1. On all other nights
we eat either leavened bread
or unleavened (matzah);
on this night why only unleavened bread?

שֶׁבְּכָל הַלֵּילוֹת אָנוּ אוֹכְלִין שְׁאָר יְרָקוֹת, הַלַּיְלָה הַזֶּה מָרוֹר.

2. On all other nights
we eat herbs of any kind;
on this night why only bitter herbs?

שֶׁבְּכָל הַלֵּילוֹת אֵין אָנוּ מַטְבִּילִין, אֲפִלוּ פַּעַם אֶחָת, הַלַּיְלָה הַזֶּה שְׁתֵּי פְעָמִים:

3. On all other nights
we do not dip our herbs even once;
on this night why do we dip them twice?

שֶׁבְּכָל הַלֵּילוֹת, אָנוּ אוֹכְלִין, בֵּין יוֹשְׁבִין, וּבֵין מְסֻבִּין, הַלַּיְלָה הַזֶּה כֻּלָּנוּ מְסֻבִּין.

4. On all other nights
we eat our meals sitting anyway;
on this night why do we sit
in a leaning position?

Uncover the matzah and begin the answers.

Uncover the matzah so that everyone at the Seder can see it. The telling of the Passover story begins with the Ha Lachma Anya.

הָא לַחְמָא עַנְיָא, — This is the bread of bitterness.

דִי אֲכָלוּ אֲבָהָתָנָא	Which our ancestors ate
בְּאַרְעָא דְמִצְרָיִם.	in the land of Egypt.
כָּל־דִכְפִין יֵיתֵי וְיֵכֻל,	All who are hungry — come and eat.
כָּל־דִצְרִיךְ	All who are needy —
יֵיתֵי וְיִפְסַח.	come and celebrate Passover with us.
הָשַׁתָּא הָכָא,	Now we are here;
לְשָׁנָה הַבָּאָה בְּאַרְעָא דְיִשְׂרָאֵל.	next year may we be in Israel.
הָשַׁתָּא עַבְדֵי,	Now we are slaves;
לְשָׁנָה הַבָּאָה בְּנֵי חוֹרִין.	next year may we all be free.

The Seder ceremony is a time for Torah study and discussion. The learning session starts with the youngest child asking the Four Questions—"Mah Nishtanah."

מַגִּיד
MAGID
Telling

The fifth ceremony of the Seder is called Magid, the telling of the Passover story.

You start by reciting the prayer Ha Lachma Anya. This prayer was written about 1600 years ago in Babylon, where thousands of Jews lived. The prayer is written in Aramaic, the language of Babylon. The prayer was written in Aramaic so that all the people could understand it.

In this prayer we thank God for all the blessings that we enjoy. We also invite people less fortunate than us to join us at the Seder.

The Ha Lachma Anya prayer talks about Lechem Oni, the poor man's bread.

Matzah is Lechem Oni because it is pale and white like a poor person who has had very little to eat and works hard from morning till night. Like poor man's bread it is made only with flour, without nourishing ingredients like eggs and milk. And, like poor man's bread, it is hard to eat and digest.

Why do we recite the Ha Lachma Anya at the Seder? Because Passover is also known as the Festival of Freedom. On Passover we celebrate the freeing of the slaves from Egypt. When we recite this prayer we also remind ourselves that there are still many people who are poor and who live as slaves.

Today, a special fund for the poor called Maot Hittim ("money for wheat") is collected and distributed before Passover.

It is a mitzvah to share with others. Helping and sharing is something God wants us to do. When we share we are making the world a better place in which to live.

יַחַץ
YAHATZ
Breaking Matzah

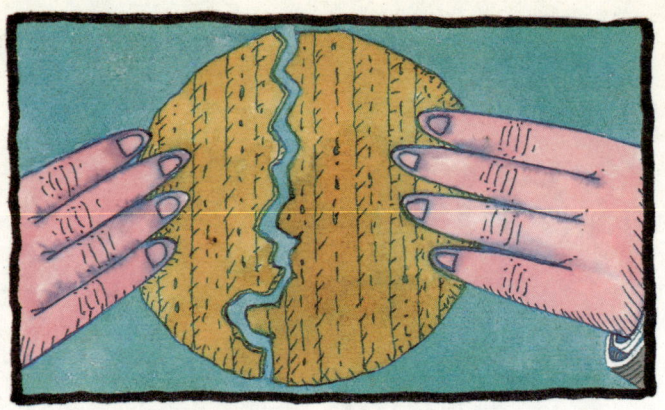

The fourth ceremony of the Seder is Yahatz, the breaking of the middle matzah.

Near the K'arah is a special matzah holder. The matzah holder has three matzot. Some say that the three matzot are for the three kinds of Jews that have existed since the days of the Bible:

Kohen—the Priest
Levi—the Levite
Yisrael—the Israelite

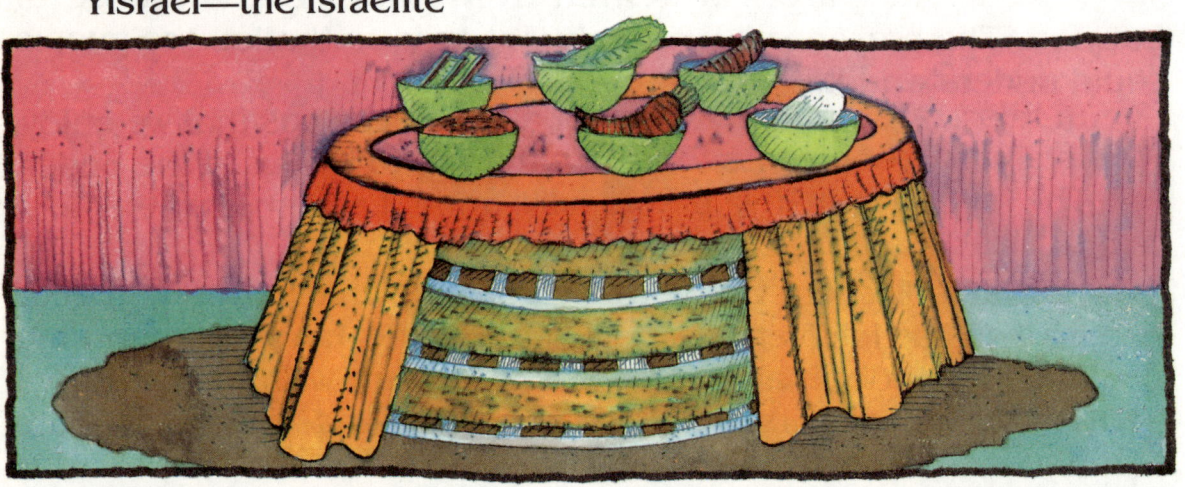

The leader breaks the middle matzah. One half is replaced into the matzah holder. The other half is wrapped in a napkin and becomes the Afikomen.

The word Afikomen, in Greek, means "dessert." The Afikomen is eaten at the end of the meal as a dessert.

At this point in the Seder the leader hides the Afikomen.

The Seder cannot be completed without the Afikomen. Returning the Afikomen is a happy time. When you give the Afikomen back to the leader, so that the Seder can be continued, you will get a special present.

The leader of the Seder breaks the middle matzah. Leaving half of it in the matzah holder, the leader hides the other half till after dinner, for the Afikomen.

כַּרְפַּס
KARPAS
Greens

The third ceremony of the Seder is known as Karpas.

The Karpas is a vegetable such as parsley or potatoes. At the Seder, the Karpas is dipped in salt water and eaten after the recitation of a blessing.

Why do we eat Karpas at the Seder? Because Passover is also known as Hag Ha-Aviv, the Spring Festival. The Karpas reminds us of our ancestors who lived in the ancient land of Israel. Passover was a happy time and marked the beginning of the barley harvest.

The leader of the Seder takes some parsley, or any other vegetable, dips it into salt-water, and distributes some to everyone at the table.

Before we eat the Karpas we say:

בָּרוּךְ אַתָּה יְיָ, **Blessed is Adonai,**
אֱלֹהֵינוּ מֶלֶךְ הָעוֹלָם, our God, ruler of the world,
בּוֹרֵא פְּרִי הָאֲדָמָה. who created the fruit of the earth.

בָּרוּךְ אַתָּה יְיָ,
אֱלֹהֵינוּ מֶלֶךְ הָעוֹלָם,
שֶׁהֶחֱיָנוּ, וְקִיְּמָנוּ,
וְהִגִּיעָנוּ,
לַזְּמַן הַזֶּה.

Blessed is Adonai,
our God, ruler of the world,
who has kept us alive and well,
and given us the opportunity
to celebrate this happy occasion.

וּרְחַץ
URHATZ
Washing

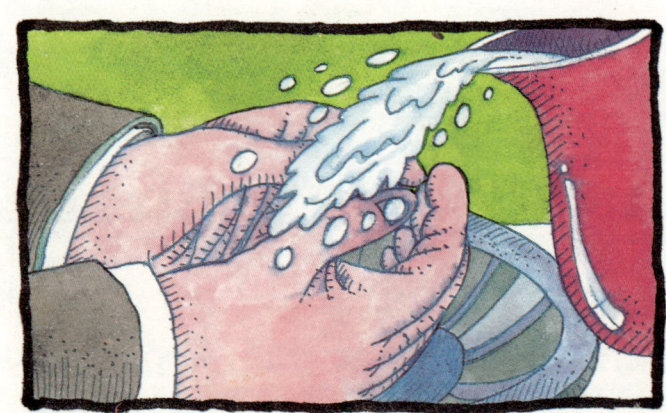

The second ceremony of the Seder is known as Urhatz, the washing of the hands.

Why do we wash our hands before the start of the Seder? Because the washing of the hands is an act of holiness which prepares us to take part in the Seder.

Wash the hands before dipping the karpas but do not say a blessing. The ceremony may be performed at the table with a glass and a bowl.

(לשבת וְשַׁבָּת) וּמוֹעֲדֵי קָדְשֶׁךָ	You gave us (Shabbat and) holy festivals
(לשבת בְּאַהֲבָה וּבְרָצוֹן)	(with love)
בְּשִׂמְחָה וּבְשָׂשׂוֹן	with happiness
הִנְחַלְתָּנוּ:	and with joy.
בָּרוּךְ אַתָּה יְיָ,	Blessed is Adonai,
מְקַדֵּשׁ (לשבת הַשַּׁבָּת וְ)	who makes holy (Shabbat and),
יִשְׂרָאֵל וְהַזְּמַנִּים.	Israel, and all the seasons.

On Saturday night say:

בָּרוּךְ אַתָּה יְיָ, **Blessed is Adonai,**
אֱלֹהֵינוּ מֶלֶךְ הָעוֹלָם, our God, ruler of the world,
בּוֹרֵא, מְאוֹרֵי הָאֵשׁ. creator of light and fire.

בָּרוּךְ אַתָּה יְיָ, **Blessed is Adonai,**
אֱלֹהֵינוּ מֶלֶךְ הָעוֹלָם, our God, ruler of the world,
הַמַּבְדִּיל בֵּין קֹדֶשׁ לְחוֹל, who separates the holy from the plain,
בֵּין אוֹר לְחֹשֶׁךְ, the light from darkness,
בֵּין יִשְׂרָאֵל לָעַמִּים, Israel from other nations,
בֵּין יוֹם הַשְּׁבִיעִי between the seventh day of rest
לְשֵׁשֶׁת יְמֵי הַמַּעֲשֶׂה. and the six days of work.
בֵּין קְדֻשַּׁת שַׁבָּת between the holiness of the Sabbath,
לִקְדֻשַּׁת יוֹם טוֹב הִבְדַּלְתָּ. and the holiness of the Festivals.
וְאֶת־יוֹם הַשְּׁבִיעִי You made the seventh day holier
מִשֵּׁשֶׁת יְמֵי הַמַּעֲשֶׂה קִדַּשְׁתָּ. than the six days of work.
הִבְדַּלְתָּ וְקִדַּשְׁתָּ You have distinguished
אֶת־עַמְּךָ יִשְׂרָאֵל בִּקְדֻשָּׁתֶךָ. and made your people of Israel holy
בָּרוּךְ אַתָּה יְיָ, Blessed is Adonai
הַמַּבְדִּיל who distinguished
בֵּין־קֹדֶשׁ לְקֹדֶשׁ. between holiness and holiness.

וַיִּשְׁבֹּת בַּיּוֹם הַשְּׁבִיעִי,	And God rested on the seventh
מִכָּל־מְלַאכְתּוֹ אֲשֶׁר עָשָׂה.	from all the work of creation:
וַיְבָרֶךְ אֱלֹהִים אֶת־יוֹם הַשְּׁבִיעִי	And God blessed the seventh day,
וַיְקַדֵּשׁ אֹתוֹ,	and made it holy,
כִּי בוֹ שָׁבַת מִכָּל־מְלַאכְתּוֹ,	Because on that day, God rested,
אֲשֶׁר־בָּרָא אֱלֹהִים לַעֲשׂוֹת:	from all the work of creation.

On a weekday start here (on Shabbat add words in parentheses).

סָבְרֵי מָרָנָן וְרַבָּנָן וְרַבּוֹתַי:

בָּרוּךְ אַתָּה יְיָ, Blessed is Adonai,

אֱלֹהֵינוּ מֶלֶךְ הָעוֹלָם,	our God, ruler of the world,
בּוֹרֵא, פְּרִי הַגָּפֶן.	who created the fruit of the vine.

בָּרוּךְ אַתָּה יְיָ, Blessed is Adonai,

אֱלֹהֵינוּ מֶלֶךְ הָעוֹלָם,	our God, ruler of the world.
אֲשֶׁר בָּחַר בָּנוּ מִכָּל־עָם,	who chose us among all nations
וְרוֹמְמָנוּ מִכָּל־לָשׁוֹן,	and raised us above all other people,
וְקִדְּשָׁנוּ בְּמִצְוֹתָיו,	and made us holy with commandments,
וַתִּתֶּן לָנוּ יְיָ אֱלֹהֵינוּ בְּאַהֲבָה	and gave us in love,
(לְשַׁבָּת שַׁבָּתוֹת לִמְנוּחָה וּ)	(restful Shabbats,)
מוֹעֲדִים לְשִׂמְחָה,	and festivals of joy,
חַגִּים וּזְמַנִּים לְשָׂשׂוֹן,	and special days of gladness
אֶת־יוֹם (לְשַׁבָּת הַשַּׁבָּת הַזֶּה, וְאֶת־יוֹם)	this day (this Shabbat and this day)
חַג הַמַּצּוֹת הַזֶּה.	the Feast of Matzot.
זְמַן חֵרוּתֵנוּ, (לְשַׁבָּת בְּאַהֲבָה)	This time of freedom (with love)
מִקְרָא קֹדֶשׁ;	God gave us this holy time;
זֵכֶר	so that we may remember our
לִיצִיאַת מִצְרָיִם.	exodus from Egypt.
כִּי בָנוּ בָחַרְתָּ,	You have chosen us,
וְאוֹתָנוּ קִדַּשְׁתָּ,	and made us holy,
מִכָּל־הָעַמִּים.	among all the nations.

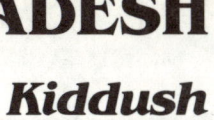

קַדֵּשׁ
KADESH
Kiddush

THE FIRST CUP

The brightly burning candles have "sanctified" the home. The table is set in "order." Family friends and relatives are seated around the table. The Haggadot are opened.

The first ceremony of the Seder is known as Kadesh, "making holy". We recite the Kiddush and drink the first cup of wine. During the Seder we drink four cups of wine. Each of these cups reminds us of a promise from God to free our ancestors from slavery in Egypt.

1. I will bring you out.
2. I will rescue you.
3. I will redeem you.
4. I will choose you to be My people.

The four promises are found in the Torah in the Book of Exodus.

Why do we recite the Kiddush on Passover? Because when we recite the Kiddush we are thanking God for making such a wonderful and beautiful world. We are also thanking God for saving our ancestors from slavery and for giving us this happy holiday of Passover.

On Shabbat start here.

וַיְהִי־עֶרֶב וַיְהִי־בֹקֶר

יוֹם הַשִּׁשִּׁי: **On the sixth day:**

וַיְכֻלּוּ, הַשָּׁמַיִם וְהָאָרֶץ The heavens and the earth were completed

וְכָל־צְבָאָם. and all that was within them.

וַיְכַל אֱלֹהִים בַּיּוֹם הַשְּׁבִיעִי, By the seventh day God completed,

מְלַאכְתּוֹ אֲשֶׁר עָשָׂה, all the work of creation.

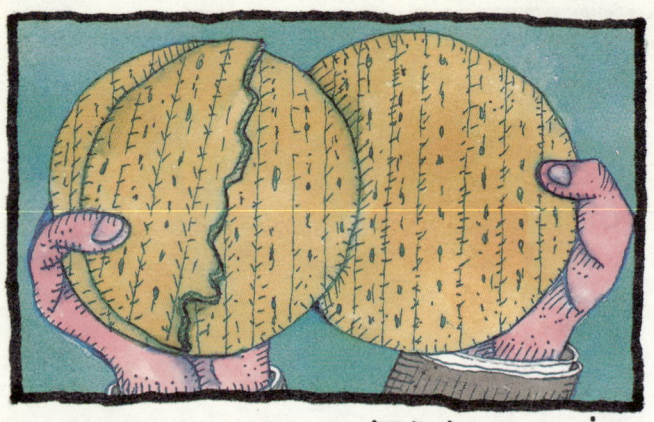

7. Motzi Matzah מוֹצִיא מַצָּה   **8. Maror** מָרוֹר

9. Korech כּוֹרֵךְ   **10. Shulchan Orech** שֻׁלְחָן עוֹרֵךְ

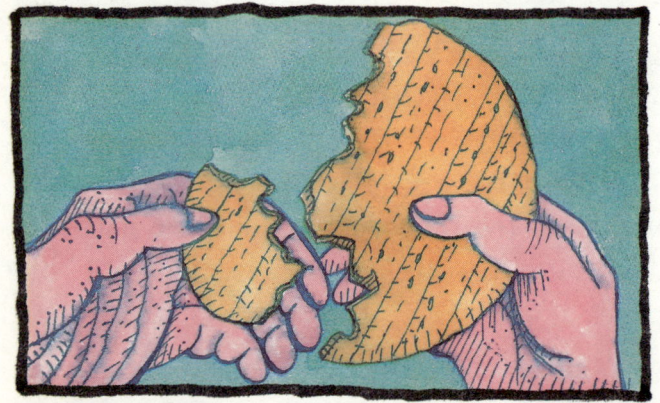 

11. Tzafun צָפוּן   **12. Barech** בָּרֵךְ

13. Hallel הַלֵּל   **14. Nirtzah** נִרְצָה

THE SEDER STEPS

The order of the Seder was set many centuries ago. Since that time the basic structure of the **Seder** has not changed since the time of the Mishnah, 2000 years ago.

The **Seder** is a happy celebration with fourteen scenes, or steps. Each scene teaches us something of Passover and Jewish history. The Rabbis wanted us to remember the steps, so they composed a rhyme with the 14 key words.

We start the **Seder** with a splash of song and we sing this rhyme.

1. Kadesh קַדֵּשׁ

2. Urhatz וּרְחַץ

3. Karpas כַּרְפַּס

4. Yahatz יַחַץ

5. Magid מַגִּיד

6. Rachtzah רָחְצָה

18

6. Rachtzah
רַחְצָה

You wash your hands and recite the usual blessing.

7. Motzi Matzah
מוֹצִיא מַצָּה

You say the blessing for bread and another special blessing before eating matzah.

8. Maror
מָרוֹר

You dip the bitter herb into haroset and recite a special blessing. Then you eat the maror.

9. Korech
כּוֹרֵךְ

You eat a sandwich of matzah and bitter herbs.

10. Shulchan Orech
שֻׁלְחָן עוֹרֵךְ

You enjoy the Seder meal

11. Tzafun
צָפוּן

You eat a piece of the Afikomen

12. Barech
בָּרֵךְ

You say Grace after the meal.

    Third cup of wine
    Elijah's cup
    Sh'foch Hamatcha

13. Hallel
הַלֵּל

You recite the rest of Hallel
Fourth cup of wine

14. Nirtzah
נִרְצָה

You pray that your service is acceptable to God.

    Adir Hu
    Ehad Mi Yodea
    Had Gadya

THE ORDER OF THE SEDER SERVICE

The Seder ceremony consists of fourteen steps or ceremonies. To simplify remembering the steps, the Rabbis composed the following rhyme using fourteen key words to help us remember the order of the Seder.

1. Kadesh
קַדֵּשׁ

You recite the Kiddush — the blessing over the wine.
The first cup of wine.

2. Urhatz
וּרְחַץ

You wash your hands without the usual blessing.

3. Karpas
כַּרְפַּס

You eat greens dipped into salt water.

4. Yahatz
יַחַץ

The leader divides the middle matzah.
The leader hides more than half of the matzah for the afikomen.

5. Magid
מַגִּיד

You recite the Haggadah:

    Ha Lahma Anya
    The Four Questions
    The Answer: "We were slaves"
    The Four Sons
    V'hi she-amdah
    Review of events which led up to the Ten Plagues
    The Ten Plagues
    Dayenu
    The Seder symbols
    Bechol Dor Vador
    Lefichach
    B'tzait Yisrael Mi-Mitzrayim
    (beginning of Hallel)
    The second cup of wine

CANDLE LIGHTING

Passover starts with the lighting and blessing of the holiday candles.

Why do we light candles on Passover? Because, just as Creation began with the happy words "Let there be light," so does every Yom Tov begin with light. We welcome Pesach by performing the mitzvah of lighting the holiday candles.

The brightly burning candles create an atmosphere of love, peace, and family togetherness.

Holding their hands over the candles the women recite the following blessing:

בָּרוּךְ אַתָּה יְיָ, **Blessed is Adonai,**
אֱלֹהֵינוּ מֶלֶךְ הָעוֹלָם, our God, ruler of the world,
אֲשֶׁר קִדְּשָׁנוּ בְּמִצְוֹתָיו, who made us holy with mitzvot,
וְצִוָּנוּ and commanded us
לְהַדְלִיק נֵר to light candles
(שֶׁל שַׁבָּת וְ)שֶׁל יוֹם טוֹב. for (Shabbat and) for Yom Tov.

SALT WATER

Near the Seder plate we place a dish of salt water. The salt water reminds us of the tears our ancestors shed in Egypt.

THE KITTEL

It was the custom, in many Jewish homes in eastern Europe, for the leader to wear a white robe and a white skull cap during the Seder.

The robe is known by its Yiddish name *kittel.* The white robe, reminds us of the priests in the Holy Temple in Jerusalem. It is also a symbol of freedom and dignity. The custom is still observed by some Jews today.

THE SEDER PLATE

An important feature of the Seder table is the Seder plate. On it are placed five symbols. Specially designed Seder plates are often used for this occasion.

In Hebrew, the Seder plate is called K'arah.

These are the five symbols:

Haroset (chopped apples, nuts, and raisins, mixed with cinnamon and wine)—to remind us of the cement our people made when they were slaves in Egypt.

Karpas (parsley or any green vegetable)—to remind us of the things that come to life each spring.

Maror (bitter herbs)—to remind us of the bitter lives of our people in Egypt.

Z'roah (a roasted shankbone)—to remind us of the foods our people brought to the Holy Temple in Jerusalem on Passover.

Baytzah (roasted egg)—a symbol of life.

Each symbol has a special place on the Seder plate.

THE THREE MATZOT

Our ancestors left Egypt in a hurry. They did not have enough time to allow their dough to become soft and to rise. Therefore, they ate matzot, unleavened bread. Today, we eat matzot on Passover as a reminder of their leaving Egypt.

On the Seder table is a special matzah holder for three matzot. The three matzot represent three kinds of biblical Jews: Kohen—the priest, Levi—the Levite, and Yisrael—the Israelite.

ELIJAH'S CUP

In the center of the Seder table is a large, shiny wine cup in honor of Elijah the Prophet. The Rabbis say that Elijah will announce the coming of the Messiah and bring peace and freedom to the world.

Elijah's cup is the fifth cup. It symbolizes the fifth promise made by God to the Israelites:

"I will bring you into the land which I promised to give to Abraham, Isaac and Jacob..."

Exodus 6:8

THE PASSOVER TABLE

THE HAGGADAH

The Haggadah is a kind of "guidebook" for the celebration of Passover. It has directions on how to conduct the Seder, explanations for the Passover symbols, selections from the Book of Psalms (113–118), interesting stories, children's folk songs, riddles and prayers. Most important of all, it tells the story of why we celebrate Passover.

The Haggadah has a long history. It is more than 2,000 years old. Even before it was written down, the father of the family would tell the story of Passover at the Seder table. He was following the commandment in the Bible, "You shall tell your child in that day, saying: It is because of that which the Lord did for me when I came out of Egypt." The very term "Haggadah" comes from the Hebrew word *haged,* which means "to tell."

As time went by, more parts were added to the Haggadah, which was still not written down—prayers, hymns, selections from the Mishnah. By the Middle Ages so much had been added that it was necessary to write down the Haggadah. But even then it was not a separate book; it was a part of the prayer book. Soon after the Middle Ages the Haggadah became a book in its own right.

WHAT PASSOVER IS

Passover is many things. It is a Festival of Freedom, when we recall how the Almighty released our ancestors from slavery in Egypt and helped a free people come into existence.

Passover is an Agricultural Festival, reminding us of the Land of Israel in the time of the First and Second Temples. In those days, our ancestors were farmers, tilling the soil for a livelihood. Passover marked the beginning of the grain harvest.

Passover is also a Pilgrim Festival. Three times during the year, the Israelites, according to the laws of the Torah, went in joyous procession to Jerusalem, there to celebrate the festivals of Passover, Shavuot, and Sukkot.

Passover is all of these things, but it is especially a holiday for children. Our ancestors were instructed: "You shall tell it to your children." The Seder Service, the reading of the Haggadah, the Four Questions, the "stealing" of the Afikomen—all these are meant for boys and girls, to teach them the importance of this great holiday in the history of the Jewish people.

PHARAOH   Pharaoh was the name for the rulers of ancient Egypt. Some believe that the Pharaoh at the time of the Exodus from Egypt was Ramses II.

PITHOM AND RAMSES   These two Egyptian cities were built by the Jewish slaves. Pithom and Ramses were "store cities," which were filled with food and Pharaoh's treasures.

SALT WATER   During the Seder we use a dish of salt water. The salt water reminds us of the sweat and tears of our ancestors in Egypt.

SEDER   The holiday of Passover begins with a special meal called a Seder. The Hebrew word Seder means "order." We call this special meal a Seder for two reasons:

    1. The Seder table is arranged in a special "order."
    2. The Seder service follows a special "order."

THREE MATZOT   The matzot holder can be made of any type of material. It holds three matzot. Some say that the three matzot are for the three kinds of Jews: Kohen, the priest; Levi, the Levite; Yisrael, the Israelite.

TWELVE TRIBES   The Twelve Tribes were descendants of the twelve sons of Jacob. Each tribe received a portion of land when the Israelites entered Canaan. The priestly tribe of Levi did not get a portion of land.

Z'ROAH   This is the shankbone on the Seder plate. It helps us remember the Passover sacrifice during the days of the Holy Temple.

K'ARAH The K'arah is a special Seder dish. In the K'arah are five special Passover symbols; shankbone, haroset, parsley, egg and Maror.

KARPAS Karpas, potato or parsley reminds us that Passover is also called Hag Ha-Aviv, the Spring Festival.

KIDDUSH The word Kiddush means "to make holy." This special prayer is recited on Shabbat and on most Jewish festivals and holidays. In the Kiddush prayer we thank God for creating the world and for saving our ancestors from slavery in Egypt.

MAOT HITTIM Tzedakah means "charity." We do Tzedakah when we help the poor and those who cannot help themselves.

Right after the holiday of Purim, the synagogues and temples begin collecting Tzedakah for the holiday of Pesach.

This special Tzedakah money is calle Maot Hittim ("money for wheat"). Years ago Maot Hittim money was used to buy wheat. Poor people used this wheat to bake matzot for themselves.

MAROR The bitter herb called Maror reminds us of the bitter slavery of our ancestors in Egypt.

MATZAH Unleavened bread. The Jews ate matzah when they left Egypt because they couldn't wait for it to rise.

MIRIAM Miriam was the sister of Moses. It was Miriam who hid in the bushes and saw the Egyptian princess find the baby Moses. She arranged for her mother, Jocheved, to care for the baby.

After the crossing of the Red Sea, it was Miriam who led the women in singing and dancing

PASSOVER On Passover we celebrate the deliverance of the Israelites from slavery. Passover has several names: Feast of Freedom, Feast of Matzot. It is also called by its Hebrew name, Pesach.

FOUR CUPS OF WINE — During the Seder we drink four cups of wine. Each of these four cups represents a promise from God to free our ancestors from slavery in Egypt.

HAGGADAH — During the Seder, we read from a special Hebrew prayerbook called a "Haggadah."

The Hebrew word Haggadah comes from the meaning "to tell."

In words and in pictures the Haggadah tells the story of the Jews, our people, who were slaves in Egypt.

HAG HA-AVIV — Passover is also known as Hag Ha-Aviv, the Spring Festival. Passover marked the beginning of the barley harvest. Three times a year, on Passover, Shavuot, and Sukkot, the Jewish farmers danced and sang and marched to the Holy Temple in Jerusalem.

HAMETZ — Hametz mean dough produced from wheat, barley, oats, corn and several other kinds of meal which has been "leavened or risen". You do not eat hametz on the holiday of Passover.

HAROSET — This is a mixture of chopped apples and nuts flavored with cinnamon and wine. It looks like the clay which our ancestors in Egypt made into bricks.

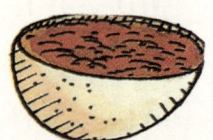

HEBREW — Sometimes we use the name "Hebrew" for the Israelites who lived in Egypt. Later on, the Hebrews were called Israelites and still later Jews.

JERUSALEM — Jerusalem was the capital of ancient Israel. Today, Jerusalem is the capital of the modern State of Israel.

PASSOVER DICTIONARY

AARON — Aaron was the older brother of Moses. He helped Moses talk to Pharaoh. As a reward for his trust in God, Aaron was chosen the first High Priest of Israel.

AFIKOMEN — When the Seder begins, the leader hides a piece of the middle matzah. This special piece of matzah is call the Afikomen. The word Afikomen is a Greek word meaning "dessert." The Seder cannot be ended without the Afikomen.

BAYTZAH — This is the roasted egg on the Seder plate. It reminds us of the Temple and the celebration of Passover in ancient times. It is a sign of our sadness that the temple was destroyed.

BIRKAT HAMAZON — When the Seder is finished, we recite a special "thank you" prayer called Birkat Hamazon. When we say the Birkat Hamazon, we are thanking God for the food we just ate.
We ask God to keep on blessing our family, our relatives, our friends, and the whole world with food and with peace.

BIUR HAMETZ — The "burning of the leaven." On the morning before the first Seder, on Passover eve, the last bits of hametz remaining in the house are burned.

EGYPT — In Hebrew, Egypt is called Mitzrayim. Joseph became second in command to the Pharaoh in Egypt. His father, Jacob, and his brothers settled in Egypt. After Joseph died, a new Pharaoh ruled Egypt, and he enslaved the Hebrews.

ELIJAH'S CUP — In the center of the Seder table we place a large cup of wine. This cup of wine is for Elijah the Prophet.

Elijah lived thousands of years ago. The Bible tells us that he performed many miracles.
We believe that someday Elijah will return to earth. When he comes, the whole world will live in peace and in freedom. During the Seder, we open the door to admit Elijah the Prophet.

Elijah the Prophet	67
Hallel	68
Kee Lo Naeh	69
The Fourth Cup of Wine	70
Nirtzah— The End of Service	70
Next Year in Jerusalem	71
Passover Songs	
Adir Hu	72
Ehad Me Yodeah	73
Had Gadya	76
From the Midrash	78
The Answers—Who Knows One	83

Table Of Contents

Passover Dictionary	6
What Passover Is	10
The Passover Table	11
Candle Lighting	15
The Order of the Seder Service	16
The Seder Steps	18
Kadesh-Kiddush	20
The First Cup of Wine	20
Urhatz-Washing	23
Karpas-Greens	24
Yahatz—Breaking Matzah	25
Magid-Telling	26
The Four Questions	28
The Four Questions Are Answered in Order	29
The Answers	30
The Four Children	32
The Children of Israel	35
Birth of Moses	36
The Egyptian Princess	38
Moses Fights for the Weak	40
The Burning Bush	42
Moses Talks to Pharaoh	44
The Ten Plagues	46
Dayenu	50
Crossing the Red Sea	54
Halleluyah	56
The Second Cup of Wine	58
Rachtzah-Washing	58
Motzi Matzah—Eating Matzah	59
Maror-Bitter Herbs	60
Korech—The Sandwich	61
Shulchan Orech—Mealtime	62
Tzafun-Afikomen	63
Barech—Thanks	64
Ani Maamin—The Song of Hope	66
The Third Cup of Wine	66

*for
four:
four questions,
four promises,
four children,
four cups of wine,
and
four super grandchildren:*
DAVID ARI SCHARFSTEIN
MATTHEW ASHER SCHARFSTEIN
DANIELLE FAYE SCHARFSTEIN
JEFFREY HAROLD SCHARFSTEIN

copyright © 1990
KTAV PUBLISHING HOUSE INC.
ISBN 0-88125-277-8

manufactured in Hong Kong

The Story HAGGADAH

by Sol Scharfstein
art by Arthur Friedman

KTAV PUBLISHING HOUSE INC.